THE

FIGHT

OF OUR

LIVES

THE
FIGHT
OF OUR
LIVES

Knowing the Enemy, Speaking the Truth &
Choosing to Win the War Against Radical Islam

WILLIAM J. BENNETT
AND SETH LEIBSOHN

THOMAS NELSON
Since 1798

NASHVILLE   DALLAS   MEXICO CITY   RIO DE JANEIRO

Published in Nashville, Tennessee, by Thomas Nelson. Thomas Nelson is a registered trademark of Thomas Nelson, Inc.

Scripture quotations marked NIV are from HOLY BIBLE: NEW INTERNATIONAL VERSION®. © 1973, 1978, 1984 by International Bible Society. Used by permission of Zondervan Publishing House. All rights reserved.

Scripture quotations marked KJV are from the King James Version.

Thomas Nelson, Inc., titles may be purchased in bulk for educational, business, fund-raising, or sales promotional use. For information, please e-mail SpecialMarkets@ThomasNelson.com.

ISBN 978-1-59555-029-3 (HC)
ISBN 978-1-59555-547-2 (TP)

Library of Congress Control Number: 2011920640

Printed in the United States of America

*Dedicated to the men and women
who volunteer to wear our nation's uniform,
and to all those who support them,
their mission, and their families.*

The names of those who in their lives fought for life
Who wore at their hearts the fire's center.
Born of the sun they traveled a short while towards the sun,
And left the vivid air signed with their honor.

—STEPHEN SPENDER

But the best of all is to let him read no science but to give
him a grand general idea that he knows it all and that
everything he happens to have picked up in casual talk
and reading is "the results of modern investigation." Do
remember you are there to fuddle him.

—SCREWTAPE, FROM C. S. LEWIS'S *THE SCREWTAPE LETTERS*

Our diversity, not only in our Army, but in our country, is a
strength. And as horrific as this tragedy was, if our diversity
becomes a casualty, I think that's worse.

—ARMY CHIEF OF STAFF GENERAL GEORGE CASEY,
SPEAKING AFTER U.S. ARMY MAJOR NIDAL HASAN
MURDERED THIRTEEN AND ONE UNBORN CHILD AT FORT HOOD[1]

If the chance loss of a battle, that is, a particular cause, ruins
a state, there is a general cause that created the situations
whereby this state could perish by the loss of a single battle.

—CHARLES DE SECONDAT, BARON DE MONTESQUIEU[2]

CONTENTS

Introduction xi

1 Fort Hood and the Crisis of Will 1
2 How We Got Here 19
3 A Year After, and After 33
4 Mission Obscured. 57
5 Changing Rhetoric, New Propitiation 69
6 The Iranian Threat. 85
7 False Peace and True Peace 103
8 The West and Islam 129

Epilogue: Beginning the Great Relearning 143
Acknowledgments. 151
Notes 155
Index 177

INTRODUCTION

This is not a book intended to detail every mistake, error, and lapse of judgment we have made in the war that radical Islam has declared on America and the West. Nor is it a book that can describe every threat against us. Nor is this book meant merely as a criticism of President Barack Obama. The truth is we have criticisms of both this and the previous administration, as we have certain praise for both as well. And most recently, President Obama deserves credit for increasing drone attacks in Pakistan and directing a surge in Afghanistan (even as his political base opposed it) and, later, for placing General David Petraeus in charge of our efforts there. Across several other major planes, however, the story is much less encouraging. Over the summer and fall of 2010, as we were completing this manuscript, we grew frustrated with the inability to keep up with the news items from the terror front, knowing that by the time this book hit the bookstores, many more events would have taken place.

Just a sample: As we were working on final edits, the news broke that terrorists from al-Qaeda in the Arabian Peninsula had attempted to place bombs on cargo airliners headed to the United States. The day before, the news from the war front was in Washington, D.C., where it was revealed that one Farooque Ahmed (who lived in Ashburn, Virginia) was arrested for plotting to blow up Metro stations in the Washington area. Just the week before that, the nation was in an uproar over NPR's firing of contributor Juan Williams for his statement made on Fox News: "[W]hen I get on the plane, I got to tell you, if I see people who are in Muslim garb and I think, you know, they are identifying themselves first and foremost as Muslims, I get worried. I get nervous."

Williams said his fears stemmed in part from the statement delivered in federal court by Faisal Shahzad (the Times Square bomber), during his sentencing hearing in early October. It was in open court in New York City that Shahzad told the judge and the world, "In the name of Allah, the most gracious, the most merciful, this is but one life. If I am given a thousand lives, I will sacrifice them all for the sake of Allah fighting this cause, defending our lands, making the word of Allah supreme over any religion or system." He continued:

> [B]race yourselves, because the war with Muslims has just begun. Consider me only a first droplet of the flood that will follow me. And only this time it's not imperial Japan or Germany, Vietnam or Russian communism. This time it's the war against people who believe in the book of Allah and follow the commandments, so this is a war against Allah. So let's see how you can defeat your Creator, which you can never do. Therefore, the defeat of U.S. is imminent and will happen in the near future, inshallah ["Allah willing"], which will only give rise to much awaited Muslim caliphate, which is the only true world order.[1]

Just prior to this event, ABC News's Christiane Amanpour hosted a special forum attempting to resolve the question "Should Americans Fear Islam?" The show would have been nearly unremarkable and forgettable save for one of Amanpour's panelists, the British-born former president of the Society of Muslim Lawyers, Anjem Choudary. There, Choudary stated to the world: "[T]his idea that you have moderate Muslims and you have radical Muslims, you know, it's complete nonsense. A Muslim is the one who submits to the command of the creator. If he submits, he is a practicing Muslim. If he is not, then he should be practicing." He continued on, to state his view of what Islam—and he—stands for when asked by Amanpour if Americans should fear Islam: "We do believe, as Muslims, the East and the West will one day be governed by the Sharia. Indeed, we believe that one day, the flag of Islam will fly over the White House."

Just prior to this episode, in September 2010, Iranian president Mahmoud Ahmadinejad addressed the United Nations in New York City, saying, among other things, that the notion that al-Qaeda was responsible for 9/11 was merely a theory and it was equiprobable that "some segments within the U.S. government orchestrated the attack to reverse the declining American economy and its grips on the Middle East in order to save the Zionist regime . . . The majority of the American people as well as most nations and politicians around the world agree with this view."*

---

* Why this country continues to allow terrorist thugs such as Ahmadinejad into this country, even to address the UN, is of continuous embarrassment. In times past, we had leaders, even at the state and local levels, who refused to give landing rights to our enemies. One remembers (or, perhaps, forgets) New Jersey governor Tom Kean and New York governor Mario Cuomo refusing just such rights to Soviet foreign minister Andrei Gromyko in 1983 when he was set to address the UN. When the General Assembly then threatened to remove the UN from the United States, U.S. deputy ambassador to the UN Charles Lichenstein said if that should come to pass, "we will put no impediment in your way. The members of the U.S. mission to the United Nations will be down at the dockside, waving you a fond farewell as you sail off into the sunset." Some eight years later the Soviet Union ceased to exist and the UN remained in the United States.

Introduction

And even since all of this, as this book was going to typesetting, a series of other incidents unfolded: The first Obama-ordered terrorist trial of a Guantánamo detainee who was moved into our civilian court system, a test case if you will, was found not guilty on all but one of almost three hundred criminal charges based on his complicity in the 1998 African embassy bombings; a nineteen-year old Muslim immigrant in Oregon was arrested after attempting to detonate a bomb at a Portland, Oregon Christmas tree ceremony; a U.S.-born convert to Islam was arrested for attempting to set off a bomb at a military recruitment center near Baltimore; Sweden was targeted by a terrorist bombing attack aimed at Christmas shoppers in Stockholm; and nine Muslims were charged in Great Britain in a plot to blow up the U.S. Embassy there (all of this, after the end of combat operations in Iraq had been announced and a great number of troops had been withdrawn from there).

From just this recent period, we can see how hard it is to keep up with events in a book that takes several months of lead time to publish and distribute. But perhaps one thing is clear from the above chronology: whatever hope and promise the Obama administration thought it could employ to soften the resolve of our enemies by, among other things, apologizing for our country's past behavior, stating we had engaged in the torture of our enemies and that we no longer would do so, trying to open more dialogue with Iran, promising to close Guantánamo Bay, pledging to move Khalid Sheikh Mohammed's trial from a military tribunal to a civilian court, and refraining from using such words as *terrorism* in the context of Islam, they had failed. None of those policies, none of that attitude, would appease an enemy sworn to our destruction. Radical Islam did not care about Guantánamo or enhanced interrogation. It cared that the United States of America was simply in its way.

Rather than detailing incidents, attempts, and the actions of our enemy, *The Fight of Our Lives* seeks to refocus the American attention on the war against radical Islam and highlight the necessity of a cultural defense of our country.

It is a cultural call to arms addressing our politicians, our citizens, our academies, our think tanks, and our schools. We focus on rhetoric and instruction as much as we do on policy and action. We focus on a notion too little heard these days: that there is a war, it is serious, and it can—quite simply—end us. And that we are not currently on the proper cultural war footing to win. Our focus is not the *specifics* of the threat and the *specifics* of our response (those books have been well written by others already). Our focus is the *nature* of the threat we face and the *nature* of the response we do not currently possess. It is a focus more on us than our enemy.

We are finishing this book in the days immediately following the 2010 midterm elections. Unlike the midterms of 2006, when Democrats made the war a major issue, in 2010 there was almost no talk of the war from the candidates or at the rallies. The main issues were those related to jobs, the economy, and deficits. There were almost no questions or comments about terrorism.

To look at the recent election, who would even know that we are in the fight of our lives? But such a fight we are in. We hope this small contribution to the discourse will help remind us, and remind us of what we need to do and, more important, who we need to be.

THE
FIGHT
OF OUR
LIVES

1

FORT HOOD AND THE
CRISIS OF WILL

In the early morning of November 5, 2009, U.S. Army major Dr. Nidal Hasan left his apartment in Killeen, Texas, to attend morning prayers at his mosque. Several hours later, he walked into the Soldier Readiness Center at Fort Hood, he sat down, he bowed his head, and then he stood up and shot and killed thirteen of his fellow Americans, plus an unborn child—fourteen in all. He wounded thirty more, emptying some hundred rounds into his victims. As he fired, he shouted, "Allahu Akbar [Allah is Great]!"

This, the second-worst terrorist attack on America in eight years, took place at a medical facility—at a U.S. Army fort—in the middle of Texas. If September 11 were not a strong enough wake-up call to the terrorist threat against us, if all the other attacks and attempted attacks failed to rouse us, then surely this attack should have jarred us to attention once and for all: there is no such thing as a safe place from Islamic terror, not abroad, and not anywhere in America.

How did it happen? How did we get here, eight years after September 11, 2001?

AMERICAN RESOLVE

After September 11 there was little doubt in any quarter, here or abroad, that the United States would go to war. After all, that beautiful fall day almost ten years ago ended with the deaths of more than 2,900 people, a greater number than were killed by the Japanese in their surprise attack on Pearl Harbor on December 7, 1941—the attack that led to America entering World War II.

One day after Pearl Harbor, President Franklin Roosevelt told a joint session of Congress, and the American people, "No matter how long it may take us to overcome this premeditated invasion, the American people in their righteous might will win through to absolute victory. I believe I interpret the will of the Congress and of the people when I assert that we will not only defend ourselves to the uttermost, but will make very certain that this form of treachery shall never endanger us again."[1] We knew we were at war that December day in 1941, just as we knew we would be at war after the World Trade Center, the Pentagon, and Shanksville, Pennsylvania. Almost immediately, "Let's roll" became our call to arms.

But now, ten years on, the lead instigators of the 9/11 attacks remain at large while the United States of America appears unsure, uncertain, full of self-doubt about the continued prosecution of this war. And how to treat the perpetrators we did catch. And

2

what to call the war we are in—if we are indeed in a war, which at present seems open to question.

In the clearing smoke of 9/11, almost none of this could have been predicted. Almost. Most Americans assumed we would make short work of Afghanistan and then strengthen our domestic vulnerabilities while closing sleeper cells and targeting terrorists around the world, if not terrorist regimes. There were places where that assumption did not hold, for example, on our nation's college campuses and in certain other quarters of the intelligentsia. Seeing the need there, we started Americans for Victory over Terrorism with former CIA director James Woolsey and others, including Charles Krauthammer, Jerry Bremer, and Walid Phares. We hoped to build the case for war and fortify public opinion. At the time political leadership seemed resolute enough, but if the public followed the intelligentsia—and the further away from the tragic events of 9/11, the greater that likelihood—the political leadership would eventually crumble.*

That is, of course, what happened.

DECLARING SURRENDER

In early 2002, as our men and women were fighting in Afghanistan, polling for support of that effort showed public support exceeded 90 percent.[2] Fast-forward to the present. As of this writing, the

---

* At the time, there were many in the media who doubted the need to fortify such public opinion, arguing after an attack such as 9/11, public opinion in the war would never wither, that we were going after a "phantom opposition." See, for example: Walter Shapiro, "Anti-anti-war crowd dreams up a disloyal opposition," *USA Today*, March 13, 2002, http://www.usatoday.com/news/opinion/shapiro/610.htm.

latest polling reveals support for our Afghani efforts to be the minority position; some 58 percent of Americans oppose the war.[3]

As the polls have changed over any number of responses to terrorism, the political leadership has crumbled. The position of the Obama administration is hopelessly confused and confusing. There is little certainty about the immediate tactical issues raised by the president's proposed withdrawal timetable and even less about the many larger strategic issues that transcend this particular conflict. Other terrorist groups and states have their sights trained on America, but from high to low this concern is downplayed while those groups and states are appeased.

The administration did not birth this confused and confusing view. One must be honest and admit that the doubts and self-doubts about America, her role in the world, and her vulnerability to it, have been building for some time. Americans for Victory over Terrorism—as with so many similar organizations and efforts—has, thus far, not succeeded. While we believe we are in the fight of our lives right now, the fight for our very survival, the fight for Western democracy, there is grave doubt as to whether the American leadership believes it.

There is a symbiotic relationship between the governors and the governed in a democracy; the American people voted in the current administration. But we don't believe that the electorate voted for military and national security surrender, not as such. Our concern is that, as things are trending, the next vote could very well be for such surrender —that is, if the present ethic of dismissal and appeasement continues. And with an enemy made bold by our dismissal and appeasement, the chances of another attack on the United States do nothing but increase.

Institutions we thought invulnerable to softheadedness in

4

war, such as the U.S. military, are already causing concern. It is difficult to say why, whether the leadership actually believes that dismissal and appeasement will work or whether it is merely trying to cope with the softheadedness of the political leadership in America. General George Casey's comments after the Fort Hood slaughter—"Our diversity, not only in our army, but in our country, is a strength. And as horrific as this tragedy was, if our diversity becomes a casualty, I think that's worse"—as well as many of the events leading up to the slaughter, are as emblematic as they are frightening.

To understand the danger we are in, we must revisit the nightmare of Nidal Hasan. We know much about Hasan and his kind of devotion today. To our shame, much was also known before the shooting. But it was consistently swept under the rug as eyes and ears were averted.

HE LOVED DEATH MORE THAN LIFE

Born in Virginia to Palestinian parents, Nidal Hasan was educated in Roanoke and joined the army right after graduating from public high school.[4] The army paid for his college degree at Virginia Tech and then medical school at the Uniformed Services University of the Health Sciences.[5] He was trained as a psychiatrist, and from his medical school graduation in 1997 until his transfer to Fort Hood in 2009, he worked at Walter Reed. Along the way he was promoted to the rank of major. He never served abroad. He was known by his peers to be a devout Muslim.

While he was at Walter Reed, Hasan began to speak out against the war on terror then waged in Afghanistan and Iraq.

Reports indicate that he worried about being deployed, but more than fear motivated Hasan. His allegiance to Islam sparked his resistance. Following the massacre the *New York Times* reported:

> A former classmate in the master's degree program said Major Hasan gave a PowerPoint presentation about a year ago in an environmental health seminar titled "Why the War on Terror Is a War on Islam." He did not socialize with his classmates, other than to argue in the hallways on why the wars were wrong. . . . [S]ome students complained to their professors about Major Hasan, but [a fellow graduate said] that no action had been taken.[6]

What of the PowerPoint he delivered to fellow officers and students? As the *Washington Post* described the event, Hasan "was supposed to discuss a medical topic during a presentation to senior [a]rmy doctors in June 2007. Instead, he lectured on Islam, suicide bombers and threats the military could encounter from Muslims conflicted about fighting wars in Muslim countries."[7]

That presentation provides a window into the events of November 9. Hasan defined the word *Islam* not—as many now do—as synonymous with or a derivative of "peace," but correctly, as "submission."[8] The PowerPoint continued for several slides with statements from Hasan such as, "It's getting harder and harder for Muslims in the service to morally justify being in a military that seems constantly engaged against fellow Muslims," and quotes from the Quran, such as, "And whoever kills a believer intentionally, his punishment is hell; he shall abide in it, and Allah will send his wrath on him and curse him and prepare for him a painful chastisement."[9]

The presentation contained several other quotes from the Quran as well, including many that he labeled as "Punishment Verses," such as, "Surely, those who disbelieve in our Ayat [verses, signs, etc.], we shall burn them in Fire. As often as their skins are roasted through, we shall change them for other skins that they may taste the punishment."[10] His PowerPoint concluded with a quote from Osama bin Laden: "We love death more than you love life."

Hasan's behavior at Walter Reed did not go unnoticed, and several of his colleagues at Walter Reed became concerned. A group of fellow physicians met in 2008 to answer whether they thought Hasan might be psychotic.[11] "Everybody felt that if you were deployed to Iraq or Afghanistan, you would not want Nidal Hasan in your foxhole," said one staffer at Walter Reed familiar with those meetings.[12]

Another Walter Reed report emerged shortly after the shooting, revealing that "fellow students and faculty were deeply troubled by Hasan's behavior," which they described as "disconnected, aloof, paranoid, belligerent, and schizoid." If those descriptions were not troubling enough, Hasan publicly expressed and shared what the report calls "extremist Islamic views."[13] He was hardly a person you would want as a psychiatrist, even less so as an officer in the military. But Hasan was not disciplined, and no action was taken—except to transfer him to Fort Hood.

SUICIDE PACT

Hasan did no better at holding his tongue when he arrived at Fort Hood. His record there includes telling his medical supervisor that "she was an infidel who would be 'ripped to shreds' and 'burn in hell' because she was not Muslim."[14]

Hasan attended a mosque in Killeen, Texas, where he was befriended by and counseled a young Muslim convert who was fascinated with and spoke on behalf of violent jihad.[15] After the massacre, that same convert told the press that he could not condemn what Hasan did. "In the Koran, it says you are not supposed to have alliances with Jews or Christians," he said, "and if you are killed in the military fighting against Muslims, you will go to hell."[16]

If sirens weren't screaming with all this, there was more. Hasan made personal business cards. They mentioned no affiliation with the United States military, but underneath his name on the cards, he listed his affiliation—his profession—as "SOA," or "Soldier of Allah," an acronym frequently used on jihadist Web sites, sites on which he was a regular visitor.[17] And finally, Hasan was in frequent e-mail contact with Anwar al-Awlaki, a radical Muslim cleric who had already been implicated in at least two other terrorist attempts in America and had since fled to Yemen.[18]

We need to pause to explain just who Anwar al-Awlaki is. Aside from having long ties to Hasan, whom al-Awlaki called a "hero" after the Fort Hood rampage, the American-born cleric also led mosques in San Diego and Virginia where three of the September 11, 2001, hijackers frequented and prayed. Amazingly at one point, just after 9/11, he was a "go-to" Muslim cleric for many in the media. Searching the news from the months following 9/11 reveals several interviews with al-Awlaki, someone the press considered moderate and reasonable. Al-Awlaki spoke variously about the attacks, against the terrorists, and about the need for justice. It should be noted that he also criticized the U.S. position on Israel and talked about the difficulty Muslims in America had in being loyal to the United States given the deaths of Muslims in Afghanistan.

Not that he had any intention of being loyal himself.

Al-Awlaki has been implicated in several terrorist attacks in the United States before Fort Hood and several others since, including the attempted bombing of a Northwest Airlines flight over Detroit on Christmas Day in 2009. The FBI was aware of, and concerned with, some of his activities and interviewed the cleric on several occasions prior to his fleeing, though nothing more was done, providing him opportunity to flee. Al-Awlaki is now on both the lam and the National Security Agency's "capture or kill" list.

That al-Awlaki could be taken seriously by the media in the days and weeks after September 11, 2001, is a great irony today, but less difficult to explain than the fact that he could be interviewed several times by the FBI and let go unmonitored, and that he could be seen as a mainstream Muslim leader in America for so long.

And all of this is just a little less disturbing than the fact that once he was known as a terrorist leader, he could engage in multiple overseas e-mails with a Muslim officer in the U.S. military with seeming impunity and little investigation of that officer, even knowing of that officer's odd views (to say the least) about America and Islam. For all the *Sturm und Drang* about the violations of civil liberties of Muslims in America—or the monitoring of overseas conversations by the NSA—Muslims in America enjoy and enjoyed civil liberties like nowhere else. And there seems to be no better proof of Supreme Court justice Robert Jackson's worry that our Bill of Rights not become a suicide pact.

Despite the many red, glaring, and electrified warning signs, Hasan perpetrated the Fort Hood attack, and no one stopped it until it was too late.

THE LEADING BLIND

Few of Hasan's relevant activities or statements were hidden events or private conversations; almost all of them were in the open. Indeed, short of calling a radio show or taking a megaphone to the top of Walter Reed, these statements were as public as Hasan could possibly make them.[19] And yet, even after the massacre, his motives remain a strange curiosity at the highest levels of government. Even today.

On the Sunday following the attack, army chief of staff General George Casey was asked by *Meet the Press* host David Gregory about the possible "backlash against our Muslim soldiers, who are in the [a]rmy." Said Casey in response, "Our diversity, not only in our army, but in our country, is a strength. And as horrific as this tragedy was, if our diversity becomes a casualty, I think that's worse."[20] Loss of diversity is worse than a horrific slaughter—the deliberate killing of fourteen innocents—according to an American four-star general, the army chief of staff, no less.

For years, many conservatives, and indeed many liberals, have been concerned about academic notions of diversity, particularly the political and social assumptions the word has been made to carry. In education admissions, as in corporate hiring, the term has come to stand for a crude notion of sampling—to admit or hire people from races or gender other than white and male.

To be sure, a goal to achieve a mixed education system and workforce in a multicultural and multinational America makes its own sense, despite appropriate complaints and questions about how we achieve such a goal. But here, the head of the army had taken this liberal notion, applied it to the military, to American safety and national security, and then elevated it above the very purpose of the military. Worse, the army chief of staff put diversity on a higher moral plane than innocent life—something we doubt even most college admission counselors or corporate human resource officers would do.

In the wake of the Fort Hood massacre, then, the first and last line of defense in our national safety renounced any notion of ethical triage. If it was passing curious how someone like Nidal Hasan could exist in the U.S. military despite all of his fifth columnist statements, here was a clue: the cultural ideology of the day had already taken root at the highest and hardest levels in America. Not long ago, this would have been unheard-of. Indeed to many still, the U.S. military is seen and esteemed not as a place of social experimentation or even elite acculturation, but rather as something rather unique that stands athwart and even in opposition to such trends.

The political historian Michael Barone puts it best in his distinction between what he calls *Hard* and *Soft* America. Hard America, as Barone defines, is "a part of American life subject to competition and accountability; [where, for example,] the military trains under live fire." He describes the U.S. military as "the strongest and most agile military the world has ever seen." On the other hand, Soft America, where Barone points to our education system as the prime example, "seeks to instill self-esteem."[21]

The Fort Hood massacre, and maybe even the very cause of the massacre itself, implies that this understanding, this once necessary dichotomy, has become outdated—or rather that the lines of division in our culture have become blurred. The soft has corrupted and eroded the hard.

General Casey's comment is not an isolated indicator of this phenomenon. We wish it were. We wish there were a retraction or clarification for the record. Instead there was only amplification.

LESSONS UNLEARNED

The Pentagon, as one would expect, created an after-action investigation into the causes and problems that led to the Fort Hood massacre.

Protecting the Force: Lessons from Fort Hood was released in January 2010, and we were hopeful it would address the lapses that could allow for a Nidal Hasan to move through the ranks of the U.S. military even as he condemned it, even as his words and actions cut through the common stake and purpose of our national defense and justified—indeed, threatened—the killing of his own countrymen in the name of Allah. But issuing a report detailing just what kind of "soldier" Hasan was—let alone how other soldiers should act to prevent such a thing from ever happening again—was not something our military did.[22]

In its eighty-six pages, not once does the report actually mention Hasan's name. Instead he is referred to simply, almost indeterminately, as "a gunman," just like any other random perpetrator of homicide.[23] But Hasan's name is not the most glaringly absent name, phrase, or term in the report. The word *Islam* appears once, not in the main body of the report, but buried in an endnote in the title of one of many scholarly papers cited in the report. The word *Muslim* appears nowhere in the report; neither do the words *jihad* or *Middle East*. "There are two basic problems with the grotesque non-report on the Islamist-terror massacre at Fort Hood," said military analyst Lieutenant Colonel (Ret.) Ralph Peters. "It's not about what happened at Fort Hood. It avoids entirely the issue of why it happened."[24]

In reading the report, one is practically forced to ask if it were even written with the Fort Hood massacre in mind. It seems to address everything but what actually happened. What's worse, it recommends a panoply of academic investigations and learning that seems wholly unrelated to preventing what happened from happening again. For example, in its discussion on "Indicators That DoD Personnel May Become a Danger to Themselves or Others," the report states:

> Different disciplines (e.g., psychology, sociology, biology, the-
> ology) offer varying perspectives regarding why some people
> resort to violence. These include genetic and biological causes;
> specific mental illnesses and personality disorders; reactions
> to medications or substance abuse; religion, social, and politi-
> cal motivations; and environmental factors. The causes of
> violence do not fall neatly into discrete categories, and several
> factors may combine to trigger violent behaviors.[25]

So what to do? The report answers:

> The Department of Defense needs to understand and be pre-
> pared for the wide range of motivations and methods, including
> self-radicalization, distress over relationship problems, associa-
> tion with hate groups, and resentment over perceived personal
> and professional slights by others within the organization.

This is the kind of revelation that will prevent similar trag-
edies? Sure, different disciplines address violence differently. But

Nidal Hasan, by any accounting of what he said and did, did not suffer from a genetic disposition toward violence any more than he suffered an adverse reaction to medication or succumbed to drug addiction. Yes, there certainly was a "religion" problem, but it is not to be included with other hypotheticals here, such as mental illness. And yes, there was "self-radicalization," but "to what" we do not know from the report and it certainly was not self-radicalization due to a "relationship problem" or an association with a "hate group" such as the Ku Klux Klan.

The report was a studiously exquisite effort to whitewash what actually happened and what actually caused the problem. What we received was a learned discourse on modern psychology. Note the report's disquisition on "Risk Factors." We learn that "[t]he range of contributing factors for different types of violence is diverse" and can include "low self-esteem, depression, and anger."[26] The report then goes on to discuss "workplace violence," "disgruntled employee syndrome," and "the employee who goes postal."[27] Other factors that may motivate domestic terrorism are, says the report, "diverse, and include animal rights, environmentalism, nationalism, white supremacy, religious causes, and right-wing politics."

It hardly bears noting that Nidal Hasan was not consumed with animal rights, environmentalism, nationalism, or white supremacy. Religious causes? Yes. Right-wing politics? It is not too controversial a point that opposition to the wars in Iraq and Afghanistan were (and are) primarily the causes of left-wing and liberal activists.

This report is not a bad joke. It is an official publication of the secretary of defense and a commission that included a former secretary of Veterans Affairs, a former chief of Naval Operations, three other admirals, a general in the U.S. Air Force, two colonels in the U.S. Air Force, two generals from the Marine Corps, a general in the U.S. Army, and a rear admiral from the Coast Guard.[28] What better composite or sample of "Hard America" could there be than this? And yet the entire narrative was skewed (and one has to presume deliberately so) to fit the government's agenda—which is simply and apparently to eliminate any significant reference to the enemy we face. What could they have been thinking?

Here is all that is necessary to say of Nidal Hasan. It is what every rational observer of what happened can see. It is what almost every news report about the incident took up in its examination of what happened, as concisely summarized by Ralph Peters:

> Hasan's superiors feared—correctly—that any attempt to call attention to [Hasan's] radicalism or to prevent his promotion would backfire on them, destroying their careers, not his. Hasan was a protected-species minority. Under the PC tyranny of today's armed services, no non-minority officer was going to take him on.[29]

The Fort Hood massacre and its official report places in sharp relief a larger and more ominous point, the point, in fact, of this book: *through our cultural and political actions, we are not now as a country on a serious war footing against our enemies, Islamist terrorists; but, rather, we are abnegating the cultural, policy, and rhetorical responsibilities of rational self-defense.*

CRISIS OF WILL

In August 2010 the Department of Defense unveiled a "Follow-on Review" with "Final Recommendations" to the initial report. Said the official press release: "The tragic shooting of military personnel at Fort Hood in November 2009 underscored the need for the DoD to review its approach to force protection and to broaden its force protection policies, programs, and procedures to go beyond their traditional focus on hostile external threats."[30] Identifying *internal* threats would be the most effective solution, given what happened. But item after item dances around the real issue.

One wonders in amazement at the report's concluding recommendation: "Ensuring that we provide top quality health care to our service-members and our healthcare providers through the hiring of additional healthcare providers—particularly in the mental health field—and ensuring that healthcare providers receive appropriate post-deployment respite and dwell time." The Fort Hood massacre had, of course, nothing to do with this, including anything relevant to "health care" or "post-deployment" respite time. Hasan was never deployed anywhere. As one major press outlet concluded of this final review: "The report provides scant information . . . on how the security lapses contributed to the Fort Hood shootings."[31] And by the way, Hasan was a health care provider.

In a more honest time, a more serious examination of the Fort Hood massacre could have been written in one page, and with all the candor and honesty it—and our enemies—deserved. It could have been something like this:

> An Islamic terrorist was raised in the United States and, because of political correctness, was given a pass throughout his professional career in the United States military. His allegiance was not to his country but to his radical religion. He told his colleagues of this again and again. He didn't set off signals; he set off sirens. And nothing was done. The military

leadership didn't take his words seriously, even as we were at war with people saying the exact same things he was saying. And the culture of the army that coddled him was too well represented by the army chief of staff who, after the rampage, said, "As horrific as this tragedy was, if our diversity becomes a casualty, I think that's worse."

It was exactly this thinking that led to us keeping Major Hasan in the army and that diminished and reduced force protection. Worse, it was this culture that allowed an Islamist terrorist into the army. Worse yet, it was this political correctness that led to the deaths of American innocents.

By criticizing the leadership of our military, the political leadership, we in no way mean to impugn the hundreds of thousands of excellent and dedicated uniformed personnel of our military, or for that matter, the loyal Muslims now serving, who had nothing to do with the Pentagon report or the political decisions to cast our fight as other than what it is. Many of these men and women have, in fact, stated their disagreement with this new political turn of events both on and off the record. It is political leadership that has plunged us into our present crisis of will.

And by dwelling on Fort Hood we by no means wish to discount or ignore the many other failures and lapses that have put our citizens and servicemen at risk—and in some cases have ended their lives. Fort Hood and the resultant reports serve as emblems of the larger point: if we want to prevent another slaughter, we must end this infection of the mind where we no longer call things by their proper names. That this was not prevented is a shame on our institutions and indicative of a preemptive cultural surrender that we never thought would affect the U.S. military or any other level of government after September 11, 2001, but sadly—dangerously—it has.

The bottom line is this: the words *Islam, terrorism,* or even their modified forms such as *radical Islam,* and the violence that these philosophies fuel, are being shunted aside, made ineffable, quieted, and hushed from high to low. Americans and her allies—indeed, almost anyone in radical Islam's way—are being targeted, have been for a long time, and it is not letting up. Sadly it is we, in our rhetoric and mind-set, who are letting up.

This tendency goes back further than most think and will reap a whirlwind that we are currently ill-prepared to endure. As Abraham Lincoln put it, "If destruction be our lot, we must ourselves be its author and finisher. As a nation of freemen, we must live through all time, or die by suicide."

2

HOW WE GOT HERE

F ort Hood happened from a confluence of many things fall-
ing apart. Most of them our doing—from intellectual, to
rhetorical, to moral confusion.

After the attacks of September 11, 2001, there was tremendous
resolve in this country, just as there had been after Pearl Harbor
when countless heroes dissembled about their birthdays so as to
join the war effort against the Axis powers. Of course, America had
no military draft in 2001 but, rather, an all-volunteer, professional
military. Many who had not previously thought of joining the
military did so after 9/11, leaving careers in banking and finance
and teaching and accounting and acting and almost every other
kind of job, in many cases trading six-figure salaries for something
they deemed more important, some even rejoining the military
after having done previous duty and thinking they were going to
spend the rest of their lives as civilians.[1]

There were other indicators of cultural health just after 9/11 as well. We saw reports of people putting off their divorces, we saw an uptick in Bible sales, and we saw more and more people with addiction problems trying to get sober. We saw flag pins on lapels; we saw more flags on porches. We saw and heard better music. We all engaged in more volunteerism. And we saw something else too: the end of the sophisticated but hollow argument that matters of right and wrong were merely matters of opinion, of personal preference, of one's own taste. On September 11, and for a short period after, the face and hand of evil were evident for all to see—or, more honestly, for *most* to see.

THE ANXIOUS PROPITIATORS

There were some sophisticates who made arguments that "we had this coming," or that we were partly to blame (if not, in some cases, fully to blame), that "chickens had come home to roost" or that our support for Israel brought this on us.* Indeed, one grow-

---

* We could list several examples, but for now, keep in mind, just by way of illustration, there was such commentary early on. For example, the philosopher and author Susan Sontag wrote in the *New Yorker* in its first issue after 9/11: "The unanimously applauded, self-congratulatory bromides of a Soviet Party Congress seemed contemptible. The unanimity of the sanctimonious, reality-concealing rhetoric spouted by American officials and media commentators in recent days seems, well, unworthy of a mature democracy. . . . Those in public office have let us know that they consider their task to be a manipulative one." Just after 9/11, Columbia professor Eric Foner wrote that the use of the word *evil* to describe our enemies presented a "Manichean vision of the world, so deeply rooted in our Puritan past and evangelical present . . . daily reinforced by the media as an emblem of national resolve." Professor Edward Said, also of Columbia, wrote: "What is encouraging is the slow emergence of dissent, petitions for peaceful resolution and action, a gradually spreading, if still very spotty and relatively low-key demand for alternatives to further bombing and destruction." And of course there was Jeremiah Wright, Barack Obama's former pastor, who said, "We have supported state terrorism against the Palestinians and black South Africans, and

ing popular politician and professor in Chicago would publish the
following on September 19, 2001:

> The essence of this tragedy, it seems to me, derives from a fun-
> damental absence of empathy on the part of the attackers: an
> inability to imagine, or connect with, the humanity and suf-
> fering of others. Such a failure of empathy, such numbness to
> the pain of a child or the desperation of a parent, is not innate;
> nor, history tells us, is it unique to a particular culture, religion,
> or ethnicity. It may find expression in a particular brand of
> violence, and may be channeled by particular demagogues or
> fanatics. Most often, though, *it grows out of a climate of poverty
> and ignorance, helplessness and despair* [emphasis added].
>
> We will have to make sure, despite our rage, that any U.S.
> military action takes into account the lives of innocent civil-
> ians abroad. We will have to be unwavering in opposing bigotry
> or discrimination directed against neighbors and friends of
> Middle Eastern descent. Finally, we will have to devote far more
> attention to the monumental task of raising the hopes and pros-
> pects of embittered children across the globe—children not
> just in the Middle East, but also in Africa, Asia, Latin America,
> Eastern Europe and within our own shores.[2]

That politician and professor is our current president.

In time—months really, several months—many voicing these
kinds of sentiments would multiply, and then in more time we
would even see the argument that 9/11 was some kind of hoax or

---

now we are indignant because the stuff we have done overseas is now brought right
back to our own front yards. . . . America's chickens are coming home to roost."

conspiracy perpetrated, physically perpetrated, by our very own government. But most of the country did not hold any of these views in the immediate aftermath of 9/11. That would change, and aside from the "hoax" or "conspiracy" effort of the argument, such sentiments would become not only an acceptable series of positions in learned societies or classrooms but a very common and dominant argument almost everywhere else as well. The sentiments that were ignored or mocked just after 9/11 became mainstream—and worse.

And this, sad to say, was not all the fault of the intellectual class or the elite thinkers outside of the government or even exclusively from the left. Even in the early days after 9/11, certain rhetorical and political efforts began to show a weakening of resolve, just as there were other moments in our history, prior to 9/11, where we showed a weakening of resolve in the face and threat of Middle Eastern nationalist and Islamist terror.

The Islam and Middle East scholar Bernard Lewis has a phrase for such weakness against such terrorism—"anxious propitiation"—and he explains that such appeasement is the worst thing we can show terrorists, the worst thing we can show them if we value our safety and their reticence. But our recent history with terrorism is not a very good record on this score, and Osama bin Laden's words haunt us and remind us of this again and again, going back to at least 1983.

INACTION SPEAKS LOUDER THAN WORDS

In his first declaration of war against the United States in 1996, Osama bin Laden spoke of how we fled Beirut after Hezbollah attacked us there in 1983 (and later, how we fled Somalia) as proof of America's "fears" and weakness.[3] He returned to our fleeing Beirut and Somalia again in a 1998 interview with ABC's John Miller, saying they were proof of our weakness: "We have seen in the last decade the decline of the American government and the weakness of the American soldier who is ready to wage Cold Wars and unprepared to fight long wars."[4] And he has spoken of what the Muslim fundamentalist generally respects as a "strong horse," especially in comparison to its opposite: "When people see a strong horse and a weak horse, by nature, they will like the strong horse."[5]

This should be nothing particularly surprising when it comes to fighting tyrants—generally they thrive on weakness. What is surprising is our history, both before and after 9/11, in how much of a political weak horse we have represented and how powerfully *that* message resonated with the fanatical forces aligned against us.

It is popular and right to credit President Ronald Reagan with his staunch stand against the Soviet Union. His was not a popular position in most foreign-policy circles, and he was proven right and those circles woefully wrong. He was resolute and he was focused. And our world has been made immeasurably safer, and millions of citizens were given their freedom, because of his resolve and focus. His presidency, sadly, took less seriously the emerging threat from radical Islam and Arab nationalism. As Norman Podhoretz noted, after the second Marine barracks bombing in 1983, Reagan "signed off on plans for a retaliatory blow, but he then allowed his secretary of defense, Caspar Weinberger, to cancel it (because it might damage our relations with the Arab world, of which Weinberger was always tenderly solicitous). Shortly thereafter, the president pulled the Marines out of Lebanon."[6]

The story worsens through a mounting string of events. The Lebanon pullout was in October. Two months later, in December, radicals bombed the American embassy in Kuwait, but Reagan did not retaliate. Then in March 1984 the CIA station chief in Beirut was kidnapped and murdered by Hezbollah. Again Reagan held back.[7] Podhoretz details strike after strike against the United States and U.S. interests in the region by terrorists from Hezbollah to various factions of the Palestine Liberation Organization (PLO).

The PLO, it should be noted, had been the preeminent instructor of the world in the use of civilian transportation (sometimes airplanes, sometimes cruise ships) as objects of hijacking, going back to at least 1968, and with little in the way of retaliation from the United States (even though dozens of Americans have been killed by PLO terrorists). And the PLO has been an instructor in how to gain international recognition and credibility from terrorist activity.[8] Indeed, by 1988, in the final days of the Reagan administration, Secretary of State George Shultz gave recognition to the PLO by officially opening up a "substantial dialogue" with the organization.[9] By 1993, Yasser Arafat was on the White House lawn at the invitation of President Bill Clinton.

Between Hezbollah and the PLO, many lives were taken in the 1980s, and between Hezbollah and al-Qaeda many more were taken in the 1990s. And very little was done about it, very little by way of serious opposition or retaliation. "Prior to 9/11," wrote Jeff Jacoby, "Hezbollah was responsible for more American casualties than any other terrorist organization in the world."[10] Hezbollah "made it their business to murder, maim, hijack, and kidnap Americans with the same irrational hostility they harbor for Israel."[11]

So from that inaction, and then our fleeing Somalia in 1994, and our further inaction against terrorism throughout the rest of the 1990s (some from al-Qaeda, some from Hezbollah),* and what bin Laden still saw as an instructive piece of our wartime history from Vietnam, bin Laden took note—and the lesson he learned was, in his words: "[T]he world of the infidels was divided between two superpowers—the United States and the Soviet Union. Now we have defeated and destroyed the more difficult and the more dangerous of the two. Dealing with the pampered and effeminate Americans will be easy."[12]

Bin Laden's use of the word *we* here is interesting. Without the United States' support for the mujahedeen in Afghanistan during the Soviet occupation, the Soviets would have never left; as for the defeat of the Soviet Union generally and globally, credit goes to the United States and many brave dissidents throughout Eastern Europe—Osama bin Laden and his associates were not among them.

Looking back at this history, Osama bin Laden was busy learning a lesson. Professor Bernard Lewis wrote:

Vietnam, Beirut, Somalia, one after another. The general theme was: They can't take it. Hit them and they'll run. All you have to do is hit harder. This seemed to receive final confirmation during the 1990s when one attack after another on embassies, warships, and barracks brought no response beyond angry words and expensive missiles misdirected to remote and uninhabited places, and in some places—as in Beirut and Somalia—prompt retreats.[13]

---

* See, for example, the first World Trade Center bombing in 1993 (killing six people, including a pregnant woman); the Khobar Towers bombing (killing twenty people, nineteen of them U.S. servicemen); the African embassy bombings (killing more than 220 people, including twelve American diplomats); the USS *Cole* bombing (killing seventeen members of the U.S. Navy).

Be it appeasement or anxious propitiation or withdrawal or fecklessness, the message and lesson taken by radical Islamists (and before that, nationalist terrorist organizations like the PLO) was learned: violence against America or her allies could pay off and become a growth industry. Until September 11, 2001.* After *that* series of coordinated attacks, what Winston Churchill once said about us would, at long last, become true again: "The United States is like a giant boiler. Once the fire is lighted under it, there is no limit to the power it can generate."[14]

MIXED MESSAGE

After the slaughter of September 11, President George W. Bush put an end to the lesson bin Laden had learned up until then, and the United States went to war. In his speech to the joint session of Congress on September 20, 2001, President Bush issued the words and the call that were a long time coming, and inspired by the worst terrorist attacks in history: "Our war on terror begins with al Qaeda, but it does not end there. It will not end until every terrorist group of global reach has been found, stopped, and defeated."[15]

---

* It is worth the obvious mention that the U.S. did exhibit a tremendous show of force in 1991 in ousting Saddam Hussein from Kuwait, but even that came with certain diminishing returns and messages sent: The U.S. implored its ally Israel (one of the countries that was actually victimized by a bombing campaign from Iraq) to stay out of it. And by leaving Saddam Hussein in power after his ouster from Kuwait, Hussein declared he was "victorious" in winning what he designated the "Mother of all Battles." Such a self-declared "victory" by Hussein included his slaughtering of thousands of Shiites and Kurds in Iraq, without consequence. And it was shortly after Hussein had been pushed out of Kuwait that U.S. policy then turned toward a new push against Israel into forced negotiations with the Palestinians (who, by the way, had supported Hussein in the Gulf War, not the U.S. coalition).

His call in that speech was strong, it was broad, and it was necessary: "[W]e will pursue nations that provide aid or safe haven to terrorism. Every nation in every region now has a decision to make: Either you are with us or you are with the terrorists. From this day forward, any nation that continues to harbor or support terrorism will be regarded by the United States as a hostile regime."[16] But the president, in that speech, as elsewhere, issued another resolution from America as well, reassuring to nonbelligerent Muslims at home and abroad.

In that joint session speech, the president addressed Muslims "worldwide" to tell them: "We respect your faith. It's practiced freely by many millions of Americans and by millions more in countries that America counts as friends. Its teachings are good and peaceful, and those who commit evil in the name of Allah blaspheme the name of Allah."[17] The president, and other members of the administration, went through great effort to reassert this proposition again and again, not just in the days immediately following September 11, but throughout the rest of the eight years of the presidency as well. One of the most important, and deliberate, images to this end was the president's address at a major mosque in Washington, an address delivered September 17, three days prior to his joint session speech.

At the Islamic Center of Washington, the president issued his first of many statements that Islam is a "religion of peace": "The face of terrorist is not the true faith of Islam. That's not what Islam is all about. Islam is peace. These terrorists don't represent peace, they represent evil and war. When we think of Islam, we think of a faith that brings comfort to a billion people around the world."[18] Let's be frank: the message that our war was not against all Muslims may have been necessary in those early days, but also in those early days many people were beginning to wonder just what Islam was about.

In time our culture—along with more and more of our political leadership—would forget, ignore, and sideline the statements about evil and terrorism and absorb, adopt, and promote the notion that Islam is a religion of peace. Indeed, eight short years after the attacks on America in the name of Islam (perverting the religion or not), the political leadership in this country would do away with all manner of discussion of good and evil, of Islam, or of terrorism in its every description of the violence perpetrated in its name.

How this occurred is an irony of American history, catalyzed by a people that generally dislikes war and that, equally, has always been susceptible to the arguments and rhetoric of tolerance—where tolerance and multiculturalism have been drummed into our national psyche for the better part of several decades. Additionally, we are a people loath to criticize not only a whole religion but even pernicious aspects of significant parts of a religion. If we lose the war to radical Islam, the cause will be this irony and this susceptibility.

NO PROPITIATION NEEDED

It is important to point out that Muslims in America had little to fear, even after September 11. They could thrive here, as they had, even if they openly opposed American policies. And our government and our culture bent over backward to reassure them that they had nothing to fear.

All of us have had the post–September 11 experience of either being singled out ourselves, or knowing of a relative or friend singled out, in an airport security line when and where it simply made no sense at all to do so. Who doesn't have a story about witnessing a proverbial eighty-four-year-old Italian grandmother treated to the wand? We as a nation simply would not—in an effort at certain appeasement—racially or religiously profile, and we went out of our way to make it apparent. Much of this was unnecessary, to be sure, but the fact that we did so immediately following 9/11 speaks volumes.

So do the actions of ordinary Americans. After September 11, Americans in noticeable numbers solicited Afghan restaurants, even paying extra in some cases, "in case business went slow," as one proprietor put it.[19] Characteristic American goodwill and generosity continued to flow unabated.

And the supposed wave of hate predicted to wash across American Muslims? It never happened. In 2001 there were actually many more incidents of anti-Jewish bias reported in America than there were anti-Muslim, according to the division of the Department of Justice tasked with tracking hate crimes. Just over 55 percent of the antireligious bias in America in 2001 was anti-Jewish, 27 percent anti-Muslim.[20] Now, some might argue the anti-Muslim sentiment would have been most intense following the events of 9/11, that is, by the end of 2001. But in 2002 just under 11 percent of the antireligious bias incidents in America were anti-Muslim, in contrast to the 66 percent of anti-Jewish incidents constituting religious bias reported that year.[21] This pattern would continue, unreversed—so much so that by 2010, as this country was fighting on two major battlefields and one year after Fort Hood and the Christmas Day terrorist attempt, it was a Muslim Arab woman, Rima Fakih, who was crowned Miss USA.[22]

It would have been good—in fact, a much better thing—had

there been no rush from on high after September 11 to propitiate verbally and in our policies. There was little need, and the resultant efforts toward appeasement have compromised our safety while empowering and validating people who fuel hatred. Nothing makes this more evident than looking more closely at the mosque President Bush famously addressed on September 17.

As terrorism expert Steve Emerson noted, this was the same mosque where he had personally picked up copies of the fraudulent and anti-Semitic *Protocols of the Elders of Zion*. Freedom House noted that this mosque, built with Saudi Arabian money, was the distributor of a publication that warned Muslims that "those who choose to reside in the lands of unbelief will be considered infidels and enemies of Allah if they either compliment non-Muslims or are critical of Muslims," and of yet another publication that "asserts confidently that, despite the current impotence of Muslims to expel the Jews from Muslim lands, 'generations that will come after us will certainly throw the Jews out as the Prophet informed us.'"[23]

Not exactly the "religion of peace" or the "thinking of a faith that brings comfort to a billion people around the world."

CONFUSION FROM WITHIN

All credit goes to President Bush, his administration, and our soldiers for the wars undertaken in Afghanistan and Iraq, as well as for much of the rhetoric used in describing our enemy. President Bush often spoke of "terrorism," of "good and evil," of "evildoers," and occasionally he used other phrases as well: "Islamic extremism," "shock troops of a hateful ideology," "Islamic militants," and "radical Islam."[24] All of these terms were helpful in properly identifying our enemy and concentrating the national mind.

The American left disliked these kinds of labels, this kind of phraseology, just as it abhorred President Reagan's use of the phrase "evil empire" to describe the Soviet Union. And with time, such opposition began to take hold and gain ground.

Shortly after September 11, President Bush told reporters, "This crusade, this war on terrorism is going to take a while," prompting the media to charge the administration with wanting to turn the war into a religious, well, *crusade*. A few days later the president's press secretary apologized for the term.[25] Phraseological propitiation, first by the media and then, frankly and disappointingly, by the administration.

Yes, the crusades have a negative connotation to many Muslims worldwide. But that is not what the president was speaking of. Few apparently remembered President Franklin Roosevelt's D-Day prayer, read over the radio on June 5, 1944. Roosevelt actually did pray and speak of our military efforts in religious tones, saying: "O Lord, give us faith. Give us faith in Thee; faith in our sons; faith in each other; faith in our united crusade."[26] In America, there is—just as there *was*—no need to tailor our language to suit the sensibilities of the enemy.

There were a few other rhetorical and positional examples of confusion shown by the administration—from a 2002 State Department effort to pressure Israel on its crackdown on terrorism in the West Bank to ongoing relationships with groups like the Council on American Islamic Relations (which, aside from a leadership that was blaming America for waging a war against all Muslims, was later cited as an unindicted coconspirator in a terrorism trial).

But while America and its leadership vigorously fought the war and generally spoke with moral clarity in tough and clear language, the opposition increased at home among the ideological and political left, with support from both the academic and journalist elite. This opposition, once small, planted the seeds of our current anomie and confusion about just who our enemy is—and who our enemy is not.

3

A Year After,
and After

I t is difficult to precisely pinpoint when and where the beginning of the respectable tripartite crescendo against the war,
discounting of our enemy's evil, and our self-condemnation
began, but we affix it to September 23, 2002, barely a year after the
9/11 attacks. It was on that day that the former vice president and
presidential candidate Al Gore delivered a landmark speech at the
Commonwealth Club in San Francisco.[1] At this time, the United
States and many of our allies were in the final stages of contem-
plating the liberation of Iraq.

There, the former vice president condemned the case for war
against Saddam Hussein. "The president is proclaiming a new,
uniquely American right to preemptively attack whomsoever he
may deem represents a potential future threat," he said. But the
language that struck the hardest was another sentence he delivered

when discussing the legal and moral case for preemptive war. "Two decades ago," he said, "the Soviet Union claimed the right to launch a preemptive war in Afghanistan[;] we properly encouraged and then supported the resistance movement, which a decade later succeeded in defeating the Soviet army's efforts."[2*]

In just one sentence Al Gore placed America's efforts to remove one of the world's worst dictators and abusers of human rights on par with the Soviet Union's policies of aggression, policies that were not about liberation but involved political repression. Thus, according to Gore, President Bush's case for war against Saddam Hussein was equivalent to the wholly unjustifiable Soviet invasion of Afghanistan in 1979 at the height of the Cold War. America was little different from its then-worst enemy, and by implication, George W. Bush (Al Gore's domestic political opponent in 2000) was little better than Leonid Brezhnev (America's international rival).

Al Gore was comparing America to the Soviet Union and George Bush to Leonid Brezhnev. Little, it would seem, could have been more divisive and fray our domestic political consensus more than that comparison. And without much resistance, aside from the anti-Gore conservative critique, the charge, the predicate for American evil in the war, was laid. And from a very respectable quarter.

Ultimately, the House and Senate authorized President Bush

---

* This country had gone to war against Germany in World War II, even though Germany had not attacked us at Pearl Harbor but was in league with those who, in Lincoln's memorable phrase, would "blow out the moral lights around us." Further, it was not just President Bush who was claiming Saddam Hussein a future threat but Al Gore's own President Clinton and other nations' intelligence services as well. And President Bush had submitted a request to authorize the use of force against Iraq, which was pending on Capitol Hill. Further, it would be interesting to know how Gore justified U.S. military action against Serbia when he was vice president.

to use force against Iraq—with a substantial number of Democrats voting for the president's authorization. This was not surprising at the time. What was surprising was the large number of protests, here and abroad, against the liberation of Iraq.

TROUBLE IN MESOPOTAMIA—AND AT HOME

While we now know that prewar intelligence about Iraq's supposed weapons of mass destruction was faulty (ours and that of many other nations), the left could have adopted the case against Hussein's Iraq on both or either antiterrorism and human rights grounds. At the same time, while the administration made reference to Saddam Hussein's terrorist connections and human rights violations, it certainly could have emphasized them more. Not that it was needed, given Hussein's well-publicized and infamous record. But the left opposed military action more than it supported antiterror efforts and human rights violations in Iraq when Saddam Hussein violated those rights.

What the left opposed then, and with increasing vigor and demonstration, was military action against a regime whose record of barbarism and terrorism was virtually unparalleled. We use the phrase advisedly, but note that perhaps only a handful of other countries could claim to compete with the noxious combination of terrorism and human rights violations as awful as Iraq's at that time. Ignoring for the time being the launching of missiles into Israel, Saddam Hussein had started two wars in the Middle East and had used chemical weapons on his own people. By most accounts, Saddam had killed more Muslims than any other person in modern history.[3]

Here is just one example of Saddam's manifold barbarism. His regime, wrote Kenneth Pollack, a former Clinton administration official, would

> gouge out the eyes of children to force confessions from their parents and grandparents. This is a regime that will crush all of the bones in the feet of a two-year-old girl to force her mother to divulge her father's whereabouts. This is a regime that will hold a nursing baby at arm's length from its mother and allow the child to starve to death to force the mother to confess. This is a regime that will burn a person's limbs off to force him to confess or comply. This is a regime that will slowly lower its victims into huge vats of acid. . . . This is a regime that applies electric shocks to the bodies of its victims. . . . This is a regime that in 2000 decreed that the crime of criticizing the regime would be punished by [the] cutting out of the offender's tongue.[4]

In the long and appalling annals of human barbarism, these tactics rank among the worst.

Despite the insistence of many that Saddam Hussein was a secular Arab (as if that lessened the suffering of those under his thumbscrews), he actively cultivated a theocratic image for himself and others. It makes little difference if he did so for political expediency or because he actually believed in it. Author and journalist Christopher Hitchens wrote:

> He had himself photographed, and painted on huge murals, in the robes of a mullah. He ordered that the jihadi slogan Allahu Akbar be added to the national flag of Iraq. He began an immense mosque-building program, including the

largest mosque in the Middle East, named for the "Mother of all Battles." He had a whole Koran written in his own blood: this macabre totem was to have been the centerpiece of that mosque. His party and state rhetoric became increasingly frenzied and jihadist in tone, and he stopped supporting secular forces among the Palestinians and instead began financing theocratic ones, such as Hamas and Islamic Jihad [to whom he would pay bounties for suicide-bombing campaigns].[5]

As for the United States being at war with states that sponsored and committed acts of terrorism, Iraq was certainly one of them. We just mentioned the subsidizing of suicide bombers in Israel, but there was, of course, more.

Few today remember the name Abu al-Zarqawi, but he headed an organization called "al-Qaeda in Iraq" (sometimes referred to as "al-Qaeda in Mesopotamia"). Once the war began, al-Zarqawi and his group committed hundreds of acts of violence and murder against our soldiers, our allies on the ground, and against Iraqis who had sided with and were working with us. And he was—despite conventional wisdom otherwise—living and operating in Iraq before one American soldier ever arrived there, indeed, before President Bush made the decision to liberate Iraq.[6] Al-Zarqawi (a Jordanian by birth) was not a newcomer to Iraq; he had traveled to Iraq to attend an Islamic conference in 1999 with a colleague named Ayman al-Zawahiri (the number two man in charge of al-Qaeda).[7] And there were other Muslim terrorists living in Iraq as well, long before America ever arrived, including one of the most "successful" or famous Palestinian terrorists of all time, Abu Nidal; and there was also Abu Abbas, another Palestinian terrorist, best known for masterminding the hijacking of the *Achille Lauro*.[8]

But war against such a regime was opposed and in large numbers. With the notable exception of a few, such as Paul Berman and the just-quoted Christopher Hitchens, leftists by and large stood and marched against the war. Tens of thousands of active protestors and academics and entertainers were joined by political leaders, such as Al Gore, Nancy Pelosi, and then Chicago politician Barack Obama, as well as leaders in corporate America. (One rally in New York City garnered more than twenty thousand attendees.)

In just one two-week period in October 2002, more than four hundred organized protests against the war were identified as having taken place throughout the country.[9] In time, those siding with the protestors' point of view would become the majority, and those supporting the ouster of a monstrous tyrant such as Saddam Hussein, the minority. Given his record, the latter group has nothing for which to apologize or feel ashamed. The former group abandoned its moral sense, protesting against the eradication of sheer, unmitigated evil.

But, as with Iraq, so with much else in confronting the evil of terrorist ideology and action.

THE ACADEMY CAVES

While the road got rougher in 2002 and 2003, the wheels came off the cart in 2004. Many know the long and sad story of how our legal community began taking up the defense of terrorist rights over and against America's antiterrorism laws and policies; how the journalistic community awarded itself prizes for disclosing classified national security wartime intelligence; how antiwar protestors from Cindy Sheehan to Joe Wilson got unprecedented time on television; and how fictionalizers like Michael Moore could receive star treatment at a major political-party convention.

All of this and more has been well detailed, excellently analyzed, and thoroughly documented by the likes of such bloggers as Scott Johnson, John Hinderaker, and Paul Mirengoff and such writers and legal scholars as Andrew McCarthy, to name a few. (There are many, many more, of course—some mainstream, some non-mainstream.) Less attention has been paid, however, to happenings in academia and at certain intellectualized levels of government at the time.

To take but one example from academia, covered by Paul Berman of New York University, in 2004 Notre Dame offered a professorship to Tariq Ramadan, an Islamic scholar from Europe.[10] Ramadan had an esteemed academic and activist reputation in Europe, and his 1999 book, *To Be a European Muslim*, followed by his 2001 book, *Islam, the West and the Challenges of Modernity*, gained certain credible attention for him. As one prominent profile of Ramadan in the *New York Times* would sum up the conventional academic view of his scholarship, Ramadan offers "a reasoned but traditionalist approach to Islam" based on "values that are as universal as those of the European Enlightenment."[11] Salon.com labeled him "one of the most important intellectuals in the world," and *Time* numbered him as one of the top 100 scientists and thinkers in the world.[12]

Ostensibly this was the same reading of Ramadan the faculty and administration at Notre Dame had. But there was one big problem for Ramadan and the university: the State Department revoked his visa on ideological grounds for, among other things, giving financial support to terrorist organizations and for saying things such as, "Iraq was colonized by the Americans. The resistance against the army is just," when asked his views on car bombings targeting U.S. soldiers in Iraq.[13] But he had a record of saying more innocent-sounding things as well. Said terrorism expert Steve Emerson, "Mastering the art of *taqiyya* (double speaking to fool the unbelievers), Tariq Ramadan has enchanted many with his apparent moderation."[14]

Assuming the worst of the U.S. government and the best of Ramadan, the academic world rallied. The international association of writers, PEN, the ACLU, the American Academy of Religion, and the American Association of University Professors launched a fusillade of written, verbal, and legal protestations and filings.[15] It might be fair to say the academic community was initially duped by Ramadan's works; that *could* explain their initial invitation to him.* But it was either unforgivably complacent or insidiously complicit to defend Ramadan after his full record of support for terrorism came to light. Then again, perhaps the loss of academic diversity would be worse than barring him from the academy in America.

And the contents of that fuller record? Paul Berman wrote an entire book about it, and other evidence is freely available. Here is a small sample: donations to Hamas entities, his favoring "an Islamic state in the Muslim-majority world," and his defense of Osama bin Laden in which he argued "[t]hat definitive proofs [of bin Laden's complicity in the 9/11 attacks] are lacking."[16] Even with bin Laden having claimed responsibility for September 11, and other proofs too extensive to number here, this is an extremely

---

* Other, deeper scholars, such as Daniel Pipes, were initially duped by Ramadan as well—and Pipes has retracted his positive review of one of Ramadan's earlier works, regretting his praise of it in the first place.

odd statement. To argue that evidence, "proofs," are lacking in bin Laden's guilt is to feed the worst paranoia in the darkest corners of the radical Islamist mind-set.

There is more. According to professor Paul Berman, Ramadan has written extensively—"a gusher of adulation"—of his grandfather, Hasan al-Banna, the founder of the Muslim Brotherhood.[17] It is the Muslim Brotherhood from which came the scholars such as Sayyid Qutb who inspired al-Qaeda, the same Muslim Brotherhood of which Hamas is the Israel-Palestine chapter. Hasan al-Banna, himself, supported and engaged in solidarity campaigns with the Grand Mufti of Jerusalem, Haj Amin al-Husseini, who not only worked with Nazi Germany in killing Jews but fomented the famous 1936 Arab revolt in what was then known as Palestine, killing hundreds of Jews.[18] The same Hasan al-Banna who, in some of his last writings, wrote, "Degradation and dishonor are the results of the love of this world and the fear of death. Therefore prepare for jihad and be lovers of death."[19] (If this sounds familiar, here is a reminder: "We love death. The U.S. loves life. That is the big difference between us." Thus said Osama bin Laden.)

And Ramadan's writings show a reverence for Sheikh Yusuf Qaradawi, the current spiritual leader of the Muslim Brotherhood. A man himself banned from entering the United States, Qaradawi is a leader who stands "in the very first rank—someone who has outdone everyone else in rendering the concept of ritual suicide and terrorism acceptable and even admirable."[20] Not to leave such a charge as a mere editorial comment by Professor Berman, here are Qaradawi's own words: "I support Hamas, the Islamic Jihad, and Hezbollah. I oppose the peace that Israel and America wish to dictate. This peace is an illusion. I support martyrdom operations."[21]

And then, of course, there is Ramadan's retrograde view of women. In a 2003 televised debate in France (where Tariq Ramadan was debating then French interior minister Nicolas Sarkozy), Ramadan was asked if he favored—as his brother did—the stoning of women who were alleged to have committed adultery. Ramadan responded that he favored a "moratorium" of the practice, without condemning it outright.[22] He expanded: "A moratorium would mean that we absolutely end the application of all of those penalties, in order to have a true debate [within Islam]. And my position is that if we arrive at a consensus among Muslims, it will necessarily end."[23]

In other words, Ramadan was stating the practice of stoning women should be suspended while it is legitimately debated and voted upon and that—presumably hopefully—a consensus would be reached that it should end. But Ramadan would be sufficiently satisfied, and lift the moratorium, if the Muslim community decided otherwise. When Sarkozy pounced, Ramadan refused to outright condemn the practice, saying, ultimately, to Sarkozy, "You can decide all by yourself to be a progressive in the communities. That's too easy."[24] As Berman concluded from all this, "The seventh century had suddenly appeared, poking out from beneath the modern rhetoric of feminism and rights."[25]

But here was a man, a European scholar, with a sophisticated résumé and a good many writings to his name, critical of U.S. foreign policy (everything the modern academy esteems). The sophisticated multicultural idea that we should be above making judgments about other cultures, in this case a theological one, had been firmly planted in the academy, even where such judgments would lead one to see a cultural-theological defense of oppression of women, Jews, and homosexuals—and justify

attacks on the West.* That is what Notre Dame and its associ-
ated liberal academic defense organizations wanted and fought
for; that is what too many academies want, we note, as Tariq
Ramadan now teaches at Oxford University. And now, should
academics try again in America, they can have him. As of this
writing, Secretary of State Hillary Clinton has lifted the ban on
his visa to the United States.

WHEN JOURNALISTS MISS THE POINT

Upon the July 2010 death of Lebanese Shiite cleric Sayyed
Mohammed Hussein Fadlallah, Lebanese-born CNN reporter
Octavia Nasr broadcast this sentiment to the world, via Twitter:

> Sad to hear of the passing of Sayyed Mohammed Hussein
> Fadlallah. . . . one of Hezbollah's giants I respect a lot.[26]

For tweeting this comment, CNN fired Nasr—as well it should
have. Reporters, as opposed to editorialists and commentators,
should generally not editorialize their views. But that was the
least of it. This was praise, distress ("sad") at his passing mixed
with a superlative ("a giant"), and an expression of esteem

---

* As the liberal author Bruce Bawer has put it: "Knowing little about America and
  its history, American students are easily persuaded by multicultural-minded
  professors that their country is not a light unto the nations but a blight on the
  planet and that other cultures, if not downright admirable, can be excused for their
  failings, because those failings are, for some reason or other, ultimately our fault."
  (See Bruce Bawer, *Surrender: Appeasing Islam, Sacrificing Freedom* [New York:
  Anchor Books, 2010],19.) One could add this is not just a problem of American
  students, but too many in the professoriate as well. We will return to this theme in
  our epilogue.

("respect a lot") for one of the founders of a terrorist movement, Hezbollah.

Hezbollah, just for a brief review, was responsible for more American casualties than any other terrorist network prior to September 11, 2001, killing hundreds of our soldiers and diplomats.[27] And it has not let up since then. At a rally in 2005, its political leader, Sheikh Hassan Nasrallah, yelled, "Our motto, which we are not afraid to repeat year after year, is: Death to America!" Following that, tens of thousands of Hezbollah supporters shouted, "Death to America! Death to America! Death to America! Death to America!"[28] Hezbollah's stock and trade has included suicide bombings against Americans and Israelis, kidnappings, torturing, and, on the battlefields of the Middle East, "firing waves of missiles into cities and towns, packing rockets with ball bearings designed to maximize suffering by shredding human flesh."[29] President Bush's deputy secretary of state, Richard Armitage, had a reason for labeling Hezbollah "the A team of terrorists," saying that "maybe al-Qaeda is actually the B team."[30]

As for Fadlallah himself, he was a supporter of the Ayatollah Khomeini and his revolution in Iran, and he had been accused of encouraging, if not ordering, the Beirut bombings that killed 241 American Marines in 1983.[31] Fadlallah was also impressed with, close to, and used as a bodyguard Imad Mughniyeh, once described as "the dynamo behind some of Hezbollah's most lethal operations."[32] Such dynamism included roles in the bombings of the American embassy and Marine barracks in Beirut, the kidnapping of Terry Waite, the hijacking of a TWA flight that ended with the shooting and killing of navy diver Robert Stethem, and more.[33]

But a journalist could speak of this man, Hezbollah's spiritual leader, as a giant whom she was sad to see die. Almost worse,

however, was the reaction of the journalist community to her firing. Writing in the *New York Times*, multi–Pulitzer Prize–winning
columnist Thomas Friedman argued it was wrong to fire Nasr;
although he allowed that suspension for a month might be toler-
able. "[W]e also gain a great deal by having an Arabic-speaking,
Lebanese-Christian female journalist covering the Middle East for
CNN," he wrote, "and if her only sin in 20 years is a 140-character
message about a complex figure like Fadlallah, she deserved some
slack."[34]

A "complex figure"? What Friedman esteemed in Fadlallah,
what Octavia Nasr esteemed, was that Fadlallah had certain
disagreements with Iran's increasing radicalism and that, more
important, he had said some relatively modern and moderate
things about women in recent years, such as, "women should have
equal opportunities to men and be well educated. He even argued
that women have a right to hit their husband back because it was
not appropriate for a spouse to be beaten by their husbands."[35]
As if that is enough to call "moderate" or lament the death of an
influential cleric who is on record as saying, "I was not the one
who launched the idea of so-called suicide bombings, but I have
certainly argued in favor of them."[36]

But Friedman went further. The message of Nasr's firing,
he explained, was this: "[I]f you ever want a job in government,
national journalism or as president of Harvard, play it safe and
don't take any intellectual chances that might offend someone."[37]
That's not how we read the situation. How about this instead?
Don't make absurd and morally reprehensible claims of sadness
over the natural death of a man who justifies suicide bombings.

To Friedman, the loss of Octavia Nasr's reporting was a loss
to the West, as she was someone who could explain the Middle

East's *nuances* to those of us who do not understand. Labels such as "good" and "evil" were too strong or ignorant for someone like Fadlallah and Hezbollah. Friedman did acknowledge that Fadlallah "was not just a social worker. He had some dark side," but, he said in defense of Nasr (and Fadlallah): "The Middle East has to change in order to thrive, and that change has to come from within, from change agents who are seen as legitimate and rooted in their own cultures. They may not be America's cup of tea. But we need to know about them, and understand where our interests converge—not just demonize them all."

There may be no better description of the nonjudgmentalist grip that multicultural sophistication has handed down than this. To Friedman, as to Nasr, Fadlallah was not in the most decisive respect a terrorist; he was a "change agent" who was seen "as legitimate and rooted in his culture."

Now, a question: Looking at the pedigree, influence, and regional travel of an Ayman al-Zawahiri, with his work in the Muslim Brotherhood and association with Osama bin Laden, and the likelihood that he never physically killed anyone with his own two hands, is he not rooted in his culture? Is he not seen as a legitimate change agent by a great many people?

To be fair, the change al-Zawahiri brought to the Middle East and Afghanistan is not the change Friedman likes. Friedman properly abhors it. But presume for a moment al-Zawahiri issued a fatwa against the abuse of women. Would that be such change? Would that exonerate him? Would that allow for a mere month-long suspension of the lamentation over his death? Even if the rest of what he has done and stood for was not our cup of tea?

Is al-Zawahiri a theoretical bridge, a terrorist, too far? Yes. Then a final question: Is the change needed to uproot and disrupt al-Zawahiri's influence something that "has to come from within"? If so, our war against al-Qaeda will take a lot longer than we think. Our view is that the change needed is not going to come from within certain hardened organizations, like al-Qaeda or Hamas or Hezbollah, or individuals like Sayyed Mohammed Hussein Fadlallah, but rather, through our moral clarity and the strength of our force and the lessons we teach through that clarity and strength.

MISSING THE OBVIOUS

A final word on Friedman, Nasr, and Fadlallah. Friedman's final brief for Nasr was summed up this way: "I prefer to get my news from a CNN reporter who can actually explain why thousands of men and women are mourning an aged Shiite cleric—whom we consider nothing more than a terrorist—than a reporter who doesn't know at all, or worse, doesn't dare to say."

We admit we do not know the journalist community as well as Thomas Friedman, nor have we traveled the Middle East as extensively. But the choice he presents seems to us stinted—any number of reporters could have, and did, report on Fadlallah's death, and we are no more the ignorant for not having heard from them that Fadlallah was "great" or that the reporter was "sad" to hear of his passing.

As for why "thousands of men and women" mourned him in Lebanon? It doesn't take someone born in Lebanon or skilled at nuance to explain that. It was for the same reason that thousands of men and women mourned the death of the Ayatollah Khomeini and for the same reason thousands of men and women mourned the death of Imad Mughniyah: *they agreed with them and they were inspired by them.**

LESSONS FROM THE GROUND ZERO MOSQUE

In 2010 New York–based Imam Feisal Abdul Rauf received local authorization to build a fifteen-story "Islamic community center" and mosque two blocks from what has become known as Ground Zero, where the World Trade Center was attacked and once stood. As with previous examples, the intellectual elites have willingly blinked at Rauf's background and busied themselves, denouncing anyone who peeks at it.

Cost for this center and mosque amounts to approximately $100 million, and questions about the source of funding are, as of this writing, unanswered.[38]** But the insensitivity of building such a landmark so close to the center of a massacre committed in the name of Islam drove countless Americans in opposition to the building of what is alternatively known as the "Cordoba Initiative" or "Park51."[39]

Despite still knowing little about the Kuwaiti-born Rauf (or his source of funding), several analysts who have looked into his

---

* For more examples of how much of the mainstream media—from the *New York Times* to any number of televised specials and documentaries—has whitewashed and ignored the violent and racist statements of Muslim leaders they hold up as models of moderacy and even victimhood, see Bruce Bawer's treatment in *Surrender: Appeasing Islam, Sacrificing Freedom* (pp. 114 et. seq.).

** Concerns about the sources of funding for mosques and what is preached, distributed, and taught in them are not without merit. Terrorism expert Steve Emerson pointed out: "[M]osques have been disproportionately used as venues for terrorists to raise funds, plot operations, recruit new terrorists and radicalize young Muslims. . . . And in the United States, scores of mosques have been implicated in many of the terrorist plots since 9/11."

background have discovered very disturbing things about this self-described moderate. Shortly after the 9/11 attacks (September 30, 2001), he told *60 Minutes*, "[I]t is a reaction against the U.S. government politically, where we espouse principles of democracy and human rights, and where we ally ourselves with oppressive regimes in many of these countries."

Journalist Ed Bradley followed up with that statement of Rauf's by asking, "Are you in any way suggesting that we in the United States deserved what happened?" Rauf replied—again, back in the day when most were minding their manners and pleading for the utmost respect for their religion as a religion of general peace— "I wouldn't say that the United States deserved what happened, but United States policies were an accessory to the crime that happened. . . . [The United States has] been accessory to a lot of innocent lives dying in the world."[40]

America, to Rauf, was at least partly to blame for the attack on her innocents, and some had it coming. This kind of collective responsibility, with or without justification for the negative cast of America's foreign policy, is, of course, in perfect sync with classical terrorism justification: because a given country's political leaders made decisions that were unpopular, the entire civilian population is seen as a legitimate target, anytime, anywhere. Perhaps this helps explain Imam Rauf's more recent declaration: "We tend to forget, in the West, that the United States has more Muslim blood on its hands than al Qaida has on its hands of innocent non Muslims."[41]

We learned something else about Rauf as well. He would not describe the classically terrorist organization, Hamas, as a terrorist organization. Asked directly about his beliefs about Hamas after a State Department assessment of Hamas, Rauf stated, "Look, I'm not a politician. The issue of terrorism is a very complex question."

Pressed again on this, he justified his refusal to call Hamas for what it was by saying, "I will not allow anybody to put me in a position where I am seen by any party in the world as an adversary or as an enemy."[42]

What would most levelheaded Americans conclude about an Islamic leader who believed America to be at least partly responsible for what happened on 9/11 and would not denounce a clearly terrorist organization as a terrorist organization? "Terrorist sympathizer"? "Immoderate"? "Dangerous"? But the opponents of the so-called Ground Zero mosque were put in the firing line of the intellectual left; they were called "bigots," and worse.

Two examples of many: Former *Washington Post* columnist and *Slate* editor Michael Kinsley wrote that there could only be two reasons to oppose the mosque: "bigotry and political opportunism."[43] And CNN's Roland Martin said:

> [W]hat has been fascinating and demoralizing to watch is the clear and unmistakable religious bigotry that has taken over this conversation. Critics of the project contend that they are not trampling our precious constitutional rights of religious freedom by opposing the project. They contend that it is simply in bad taste to build it so close to ground zero, and that Americans are far too emotional about [the] issue.
>
> Other words really come to mind. Irrational. Hysterical. Intolerant. Hypocritical.[44]

This is nonsense. Almost every Park51 opponent we have seen has conceded that this is not an issue of First Amendment religious freedom principles and that were it litigated as such, it would be a near slam-dunk case. As Abraham Foxman of the Anti-Defamation

League put his opposition: "Ultimately, this was not a question of rights, but a question of what is right."[45] Both right and left have long acknowledged that what may be constitutional may not always be appropriate (one thinks of pornography cases, or of political rallies at sensitive gatherings such as funerals or other memorials).

But the Kinsley and Martin slanders go on and on, and the defenses of Rauf are legion with column after column ignoring his statements and the question of his financing. So zealous were the anti–anti-mosque builders to find a dominance of moderate Islam, so zealous were they in trying to make this *not* about radical Islam, they were willing to ignore the very Islamist, radical Islamist, statements of the man they were elevating and defending (much the same as with Professor Ramadan, much the same as with Mohammed Hussein Fadlallah).

There is one more point the defenders of the mosque make, and it is an intellectual reach: that the planned Islamic center is not at Ground Zero but two blocks away, as if people were not running for their lives two blocks away from the World Trade Center on September 11, 2001. Or, as if the very epicenter of that two-block-away location was not the exact location where the landing gear assembly of one of the planes used in the attacks on September 11 crashed through the roof.[46] It was.

As this debate raged in the media, the president remained silent. For four months he said nothing, then surprisingly took the occasion of a Muslim gathering at the White House to commemorate the end of the Ramadan holiday in August to weigh in:

> As a citizen, and as [p]resident, I believe that Muslims have the same right to practice their religion as everyone else in this country. And that includes the right to build a place of

worship and a community center on private property in Lower Manhattan, in accordance with local laws and ordinances. This is America.[47]

The press understood what the president was saying; he was weighing in on behalf of those who wanted to build their mosque. The AP headline the next day read: "Obama makes clear support for ground zero mosque."[48] The *New York Times* headline was "Obama Strongly Backs Islam Center Near 9/11 Site."[49] That following day, however, the president backtracked, saying, "I was not commenting and I will not comment on the wisdom of making the decision to put a mosque there. . . . I was commenting very specifically on the right people have that dates back to our founding. That's what our country is about."[50]

Whatever President Obama believes or believed, was this later, revised view, to borrow from Roland Martin, irrational? Hysterical? Intolerant? Hypocritical?

Was Pope John Paul II irrational when he asked Carmelite nuns not to build a convent near Auschwitz? Is or would America be hysterical in opposing a Shinto temple at Pearl Harbor, almost seventy years after the Pearl Harbor attack? One can cavil about the examples, but if moderate Islam is as it says, moderate, then it would clearly not be in the business of justifying a mosque so close to the ashes of September 11, and in the face of nearly 70 percent disapproval by the American people.[51]

As to the bigotry of opposition to the mosque, or the hysteria, or whatever epithet one desires, what the anti-anti-mosque builders fail to understand is that if we were truly bigoted or hysterical or whatever, then Americans would oppose mosques—period. That is not the case. There are, for instance, more than one hundred mosques in New York alone.[52] But even then, given what we have identified in mosques from Washington to San Diego to Houston and back to Virginia, it is not as if Americans lack reason to fear what is being preached and taught in many such places of worship.

For their skepticism and opposition to Imam Rauf's mosque, Americans were treated to a cover issue of *Time* magazine in August of 2010, with the headline and cover story: "Is America Islamophobic? What the anti-mosque uproar tells us about how the U.S. regards Muslims." The question was rhetorical; the cover story was an effort to show just how opposition to the mosque was the result of a "troubling Islamophobia" in America.[53] As if Americans opposed to Rauf's "moderacy" had a psychological or psychiatric deficiency.

Importantly, there were Muslim opponents to the Ground Zero mosque, but the anti-anti-mosque elite completely missed them in their zeal to denounce their opponents. The opposition came from three bona fide moderate Muslims, two in Canada and one in America. In Canada, Raheel Raza and Tarek Fatah of the Muslim Canadian Congress wrote:

> The Koran commands Muslims to, "Be considerate when you debate with the People of the Book"—i.e., Jews and Christians. Building an exclusive place of worship for Muslims at the place where Muslims killed thousands of New Yorkers is not being considerate or sensitive, it is undoubtedly an act of "fitna" [meaning "mischief-making"].[54]

Raza and Fatah then issued another analogy: "Do they not understand that building a mosque at Ground Zero is equivalent to permitting a Serbian Orthodox church near the killing fields of Srebrenica where 8,000 Muslim men and boys were slaughtered?" Irrational. Hysterical. Intolerant. Hypocritical. Indeed.

And as for Miss USA Rima Fakih: "I totally agree with President Obama with the statement on constitutional rights of freedom of religion. . . . I also agree that it shouldn't be so close to the World Trade Center. We should be more concerned with the tragedy than religion."[55*]

Since almost all the opponents of the mosque we know of also agree with the legal notion of freedom of religion, Fakih's statement is one of a normal, concerned citizen about her coreligionists *and* her country, fully in line with Abraham Foxman's and other opponents' views of the mosque. Fully in line with what Pope John Paul II recognized when he thought Carmelite nuns had every right to build a convent wherever they wanted, but—all things considered—that it was better not to. To promote true tolerance, the case is not with those who support the building of the mosque; it is with those who think it the wrong place to build it.

Curiously enough, in a strange cultural turn of intellectual thinking, the concepts of diversity and tolerance, as we came to know them in the academy in America, were usually symbolized by the opposition to religious orthodoxies, not support of them— but Islam became different here. It became exceptional. Orthodox Islam, unlike Christianity or Judaism, would be considered the new badge of diversity and its presence and verbiage the new emblems of tolerance, worthy of utmost respect and protection from criticism.

Notwithstanding the usual liberal skepticism over religion or establishments of religious presences in the United States

---

* We intentionally leave Zuhdi Jasser's opposition to the Ground Zero Mosque unmentioned here. His heroic work will be discussed anon.

(crosses and the Ten Commandments in public spaces, prayers at high school football games and graduations, for example), the majority of the columnists and commentators on the left came down in favor of this new religious landmark. What could explain such a joining, such an affinity, between the left and its narrative, and Islam and its narrative? The one thing they shared in common: the narrative of anti-Americanism, the narrative of "blame America first," the narrative that America is more to be faulted for the sins of the world than praised for the successes in it. So, Islam: yes. Rabbis and Jews, Christian ministers and Christians: go elsewhere. As for Rauf's beliefs about America and Hamas, his first (thinking America was an accessory to its own attack) was fully in line with much of leftist ideology; his second (that Hamas is not clearly a terrorist organization) was apparently unimportant.

The fact that a Muslim leader such as Imam Rauf, with the views he has publicly espoused, could be held up as a model of ecumenical moderacy shows us where we are today.

4

MISSION OBSCURED

Despite orchestrating military efforts in Afghanistan and Iraq, conducting intelligence operations here and abroad to keep Americans safe, and making a good defense for preventing admission to the likes of Tariq Ramadan into the United States, the Bush administration was not fully immune from the doubt that was boiling upward and outward from both the elite and popular culture. The Bush administration got a lot of the war right and then blurred some of it; the Obama administration got a lot of the war wrong and then disdained and scorned it. And things important steadily grew worse.

The problems of clear thought and language were not confined to the intellectual left. This became eerily obvious in 2005 during the Senate confirmation hearings of the nominee for the undersecretary of state for public diplomacy, a job whose mission it is to "lead America's public diplomacy outreach . . . and

U.S. [g]overnment efforts to confront ideological support for terrorism."[1]

During those hearings, nominee Karen Hughes said the following: "If I had the opportunity to say just one thing to people throughout the world, it would be, I am eager to listen. I want to learn more about you and your lives, what you fear, what you dream, what you believe and what you value most. Should I be confirmed, I plan to travel and reach out to citizens and leaders of other countries and mobilize our government to do more listening."[2] What, we wondered, would she hear if a radical Muslim were candid instead of manipulative with her? She would hear, as we have heard again and again from the fatwas and the sermons, that the pain and rage, the "fear," has to do with events such as the defeat of the Ottomans almost a century ago at Constantinople, or perhaps even further back, the defeat of the Muslim Moors at Andalusia more than five hundred years ago in that interesting year of 1492.

Was more listening what we really needed? Was it going to solve any problem or win any war? We had listened and heard enough, and we should generally abjure this kind of diplomacy in favor of our own sermons about our freedoms and the freedoms granted to people of all faiths—and to women—in America and the rest of the West. One would think a reminder about the several times Americans have taken up arms on behalf of Muslims would also be a good diplomatic strategy.

When is the last time one heard an American president—or diplomat of any sort—state loudly and proudly something to this effect: "Over the past two decades, almost every time U.S. military forces have been called into action to risk their lives and limbs, it's been on behalf of Muslims. . . . [T]o assist the Afghan mujahaddin . . . during the Soviet invasion in the 1980s, to liberate Kuwait following the Iraqi invasion of 1990, to help Somali Muslims suffering at the hands of a warlord in Mogadishu, to help Muslims first in Bosnia and then in Kosovo who faced a Serb onslaught, and more recently to liberate Afghanistan from its Taliban and al Qaeda rulers," and then again to liberate yet tens of millions more Muslims in Iraq? Such a statement was actually made several years ago by Wolf Blitzer of CNN.[3] That was the kind of talk our diplomatic corps should have been engaging in. Not listening and promising to listen more. But this new ethic of weakness and prostration was, indeed, moving from the Department of State to the Department of Defense.

And its cues, at least rhetorically, came from on high.

CORRUPTING OURSELVES

Despite having run for reelection as a wartime president in 2004, President Bush's second inaugural address mentioned the words *war*, *terrorism*, *terrorist*, and *radical* not once. It was a beautiful speech, testifying to the importance of free societies abroad and the goal of an agenda that would foster international human rights—but was that the first reason men and women in uniform were at war?

In July 2005 the *New York Times* ran the headline "Washington Recasts Terror War as 'Struggle.'"[4] The chairman of the Joint Chiefs of Staff, Gen. Richard Meyers, told the Press Club that he "objected to the use of the term 'war on terrorism,' because if you call it a war, then you think of people in uniform as being the solution." What, one must have asked, did the men and women in uniform think when they heard such a thing from one of their leading generals? Did we no longer want our men and women in uniform to think that we were at war? Or part of a solution? Worse yet, did we not want our enemies to think we were at war with them anymore? The *New York Times* pointed out that as part of this new thinking, the administration had been increasingly referring to "a global struggle against violent extremism" rather than a "global war on terror."[5]

By 2006 admirers of President Bush's tough rhetoric had further cause to worry. Asked in May what he thought the biggest mistake of his presidency was, he answered that it was his rhetoric, his "kind of tough talk, you know, that sent the wrong signal to people." He added, "I learned some lessons about expressing myself maybe in a little more sophisticated manner" and that "in certain parts of the world it was misinterpreted."[6]

What rhetoric and tough talk? The very same rhetoric and tough talk that had rallied so many Americans to war, that stood against the soft language and softer commitment of the American and European left. Bush used phrases like "smoke them out of their holes," "bring 'em on," and "wanted dead or alive" in reference to our enemies, phrases that showed we would not engage in diplomatic or transnational-speak, that we would not subject ourselves to "international tests," as Senator John Kerry had put it. Combine this apology with hints and statements about renaming the war as one against "violent extremism" and one begins to see the genesis of the weariness of our own will to fight.

This was not and is not a war against extremism or even violent extremism. In some cases in relatively recent history we did not even see "extremism" as having an exclusively negative connotation. We even once believed extremism in certain things a good thing. Martin Luther King Jr. wrote in his "Letter from a Birmingham Jail" that there were forms of extremism worth lauding: whether describing Jesus' commitment to love, Lincoln's commitment to end slavery, or Jefferson's commitment to prove self-evident truths as a basis for our founding.

No, ours was not and is not a struggle against extremism. It is a fight, it is a war, and it is against a very particular kind of extremism. And we know who the enemy is because they tell us who they are. We called the Nazis the German Nazis, and we called the Communists the Soviet Communists. We should call our enemy today by what they are and who they are and what they say they are and who they say they are.

Said Ralph Waldo Emerson, "[T]he corruption of man is followed by the corruption of language." If the one truly precedes the other, our corrupted language reveals how much we have already corrupted our will to fight. This became increasingly evident in the waning days of Bush's second term.

A LACK OF LEADERSHIP

By 2008 efforts in both Afghanistan and Iraq had become highly unpopular, and, with the economy taking a nosedive, the American people were ready for a change at the top. Two years before, in 2006, they had voted in a congressional majority that campaigned on such change, including (prominently) the withdrawal from the battlefield of Iraq. How we could become so war weary against such an implacable and dedicated foe is a troubling story.

On the one hand, the administration had done a tremendously successful job in keeping America safe after September 11, 2001. And at the same time, it had wreaked a great deal of chaos and destruction against the enemy abroad (at least in the early stages of the war). In Khalid Sheikh Mohammed's words, our military response "took our breath away." On the other hand, the administration had let up on explaining the costs and causes in the ongoing war. President Bush stopped casting the vision, and the nation's vision became consequently obscured. While the mainstream media was talking about body counts and disasters, the prosecutors of the war in Washington seemed on the defensive, rarely speaking about the successes, rarely reminding us of the stakes. They were, in Ramesh Ponnuru's words, "outsourcing the eloquence" to other writers and speakers, not by order but by default.

Following the exit of President Bush, his senior political advisor and deputy chief of staff, Karl Rove, admitted the administration should have done more to answer the criticisms about the war in Iraq (especially the left-wing line that we were "lied" into the conflict) and that the administration could have better explained the war to the American people. Said Rove, "At the time, we in the Bush White House discussed responding but decided not to relitigate the past."[7] Rove continued:

> We know President Bush did not intentionally mislead the nation. Saddam Hussein was deposed and eventually hanged for his crimes. Iraq is a democracy and an ally instead of an enemy of America. Al Qaeda suffered tremendous blows in the "land between the two rivers." But Democrats lost more than the election in 2004. In telling lie after lie, week after week, many lost their honor and blackened their reputations.[8]

True enough, but that goes only so far. The partisan loss by the Democrats was temporary, as they regained Congress in 2006 on a promise to end the war in Iraq and, only two years later, as they elected a president who was the most vocally antiwar candidate to lead a ticket in recent history. In the end, the loss was not partisan; it was a loss to and for America—if one presumes a weakened and unresolved America is bad for our allies and good for our enemies. And the charge that the war was founded upon deception undermines the whole effort. If that is true—as many believe—then we succumb to a connected awareness that *there is little reason to continue the war.*

Rove did an honorable and rare thing for a public servant: he apologized. But it is important to note the point for which Rove apologized was in not answering the charges about Iraq and weapons of mass destruction. This is not the central point, not the main reason the war effort or our resolve faltered. The administration no more lied about WMDs than any other nation that believed Iraq had them, and there were many. The administration no more lied than did Bill Clinton, who believed Saddam Hussein had them. It was Saddam Hussein who lied; our intelligence was incorrect, not doctored. To believe otherwise is a tired and dismissible canard.

As terrorism expert Andrew C. McCarthy pointed out, the administration could have said much more about Iraq to bolster our resolve, particularly stressing Iraq's role in the support of terrorism and commission of human rights atrocities on a daily basis. We did not hear much of that, and the silence led to an erosion of public sentiment and resolve. Worse, in the absence of leadership, the opposition was able to tell the story on its terms. "When the Bush administration decided to highlight Iraq's WMD," said McCarthy, "it sold too short the terror ties that were the only coherent connection to the casus belli on which the nation agreed."[9] The result?

Iraq operations became "the War in Iraq," disconnecting them in the public mind from "the War on Terror." Al-Qaeda became "al-Qaeda in Iraq," not the original enemy but a spontaneous insurgency generated by the invasion. The counterfactual narrative was thus set in stone: Saddam and bin Laden had had nothing to do with one another, the "Iraq War" was a one-off over WMD, and it was Bush's invasion that brought al-Qaeda to Iraq, not the other way around.[10]

Of course, we know Saddam Hussein was a terrorist, trafficked in terrorism, supported terrorists, and gave sanctuary to terrorists, but it was left to analysts outside the administration to promulgate these facts, facts such as were found in more than forty pages of a 2004 Senate Select Committee on Intelligence, which, itself, is now mostly forgotten, if it were ever read or publicized beyond a few columnists, radio hosts, and public intellectuals in the first place.[11]

Between the hard tug on the heartstrings that a promotion of Saddam Hussein's gross violations of human rights could produce, the dossier against him regarding terrorism, and *his* efforts at obscuring his weapons programs, a great series of cases and reminders could have been made. But for the most part they were not, and, in short order, those who continued to support and justify the war on the battlefield of Iraq were the minority in America, "war mongers," and worse. And all this just four years after September 11, 2001.

LACKING A MORAL VOCABULARY OF WAR

It did not have to be this way, and most of us thought early on it would not go this way. Consider a president who led a military charge that resulted in the liberation of tens of millions of Muslims and began the ending of safe havens of terrorism in two countries, and kept America safe from further attacks. He left office with the lowest approval ratings of any president since Harry Truman.[12]

Early on in the war, political scientists Cori Dauber and Peter Feaver suggested that Vietnam's "body bag syndrome" would not affect our war against terrorism. In March 2002, they wrote:

> In poll after poll, and long before Sept. 11, the public repeatedly demonstrated that it approached the use of force with a levelheaded appreciation for the costs of war. If an operation was worth doing, it was worth paying a price. . . .
>
> Said the father of [Sgt.] Bradley Crose, one of those killed [in Afghanistan]: "If I hold true and consider precious those things which we enjoy as our way of life . . . then I've got to be willing to let my son go."

The public will support costly military operations if an administration argues persuasively that it is committed to achieving success, that casualties were unavoidable for the mission to be accomplished, and that the mission had a purpose that gave those deaths meaning, consequence, and honor.[13]

Even the parents of a slain soldier can be part of that public. But the purpose and consequence of the mission became obscured, and the tough and noble civilian prosecutors of the war lost the rhetoric battle. In a democracy, politics, in the best sense of the word, must be taken seriously, and serious policy must be backed up with serious rhetoric from the top. In this case, absent that leadership, the cause became untenable because the case became unarticulated. We forgot why we fought, which meant the antiwar contingent could supply shameful and unjust reasons for their positions. In the fog of war, those began to carry the day.

Barack Obama, then a U.S. senator in the midst of the 2008 presidential campaign, had very different views of the enemy, of good and evil, than had previously been held by political leaders of prominence. Obama was asked by an evangelical pastor, Rick Warren, at an evangelical church, "Does evil exist? And if it does, do we ignore it? Do we negotiate with it? Do we contain it? Do we defeat it?"[14] Clearly a foreign policy and national security question. Senator Obama's answer:

> Evil does exist. I mean, I think we see evil all the time. We see evil in Darfur. We see evil, sadly, on the streets of our cities. We see evil in parents who viciously abuse their children. I think it has to be confronted. It has to be confronted squarely, and one of the things that I strongly believe is that, now, we are not going to, as individuals, be able to erase evil from the world. That is God's task, but we can be soldiers in that process, and we can confront it when we see it.
>
> Now, the one thing that I think is very important is for us to have some humility in how we approach the issue of confronting evil, because a lot of evil's been perpetrated based on the claim that we were trying to confront evil.[15]

On their face, these words may seem reasonable, but look closer. Senator Obama's first reaction to a question about evil in our midst was not to consider those sworn to our destruction abroad and at home, not those who slaughtered men and women on a massive scale, often after torturing them first. His first reaction was to name a place where we were not at war, nor planning to go (the Sudan). His primary reaction to a question about evil was about the evils in America—"on the streets of our cities" and in homes where domestic and child abuse takes place. And then, he ended his answer with the implicit message that we have been committers of evil in the name and effort of trying to defeat it—a "blame America first" attitude. We can confront evil, as he said, but we need to remember that this primarily "is God's task."

Such an answer was of a piece with the unsolicited question he set out to answer right after the slaughter of September 11, when he wrote that such violence "[m]ost often . . . grows out of a climate of poverty and ignorance, helplessness and despair," and that one of our primary tasks was "to be unwavering in opposing bigotry or discrimination directed against neighbors and friends of Middle Eastern descent," and that, just as important, "we will have to devote far more attention to the monumental task of raising the hopes and prospects of embittered children across the globe—children not just in the Middle East, but also in Africa, Asia, Latin America, Eastern Europe, and within our own shores."

Apparently identifying evil and then defeating that evil done by those committed to our existential destruction was far and distant from Barack Obama's mind and moral vocabulary. His concern over our commission of evil, however, was ever close to him as it would be as president.

President Obama came into office promising change in Iraq, in Afghanistan, and in our foreign and defense policy, not to mention other areas. And change we got—more than we bargained for, both in rhetoric and posture with regard to our enemies, in regard to our allies, and in regard to the very war itself.

5

CHANGING RHETORIC, NEW PROPITIATION

W hen President Barack Obama came into office, the war was not over. But his inaugural address made it clear that our efforts would go a new and different direction. "Recall that earlier generations faced down fascism and communism not just with missiles and tanks," President Obama said, "but with the sturdy alliances and enduring convictions." He continued, "They understood that our power alone cannot protect us, nor does it entitle us to do as we please." He said, "Instead they knew that our power grows through its prudent use; our security emanates from the justness of our cause, the force of our example, the tempering qualities of humility and restraint."

Was this the language of a wartime leader? Was America simply doing as it pleased? Was it fighting this war as toughly as it fought, say, fascism in World War II? Or, rather, were we treating our enemy with a restraint our enemies in World War II never knew, including giving them a raft of rights and protections once we captured them, and refraining from bombing civilian centers abroad? Was there actually doubt about the "justness of our cause" from the new commander in chief? Did our new commander in chief doubt the cause of ousting and replacing tyrants who supported terrorism?

And just what was meant by the idea that earlier generations understood we fought and won wars with humility and restraint? Were we rounding up tens of thousands of Arab Americans in America based on their race as we did Japanese Americans in World War II? Were we executing captured saboteurs who had come to our shores from abroad as we did in World War II? Or, rather, were we treating our captured more civilly than any other nation would treat its enemy? And were we not fighting door-to-door abroad and seeking to co-opt erstwhile enemies to join our cause as opposed to firebombing large civilian sites and cities as we did in World War II? Was the historic example of Franklin Roosevelt and Harry Truman really one of humility and restraint? What of Ronald Reagan, who ratcheted up our war against communism, taking it to its end? Did he not speak truth to power and call the enemy out by name, all the while expanding our military's budget and reach?

Even a casual read of history reveals that President Obama was remaking the wars of the past in his own image—a prelude to remaking the war on Islamist terror into a new image. In his address the president went on, more specifically, to identify where we were headed, or at least where he would like us to be headed: "We will begin to responsibly leave Iraq to its people and forge a hard-earned peace in Afghanistan." Ending the wars abroad, not winning them, was the new priority.

SALES TRIP

Along with the new rhetoric of hesitation and self-doubt, there had been much talk by then candidate Barack Obama of "resetting" our foreign relations. It took very little time after he took office to see what that would mean.

Obama's first television interview as president was on an Arabic television network. His first overseas trip was to the Muslim (and the increasingly Islamist) country of Turkey. He then traveled to Saudi Arabia. Then he was off to Egypt to deliver an "address to the Muslim world" in which he saluted concepts of freedom and scientific advance and the contributions of Muslims throughout history to that freedom and advancement.[1]

Egypt seemed like a particularly strange place to deliver a speech on openness and freedom. Said one Egyptian-born journalist in the *New York Times*, Hosni Mubarak's Egypt was and is a place of "martial law, secret police and torture chambers."[2] And, as Zuhdi Jasser of the American Islamic Forum for Democracy put it, Egypt is a "backdrop of authoritarian rule that has suffocated dissent and reform . . . [it is home to] the two-fold cancer which plagues reform and modernization in the so-called 'Muslim world.' That cancer is Arab secular fascism (i.e., the Mubarak regime) and radical Islamism (i.e., the Muslim Brotherhood and Al-Azhar University)."[3] Al-Azhar, it should be noted, sponsored the president's speech.

Where, then, should President Obama have saluted the Muslim world and have chosen as a location—a democratic location—for such a salute?

Perhaps the lack of a good answer is the answer. Or perhaps one might have thought, Iraq, where they actually elect their leaders today, thanks to brave Iraqis who worked alongside brave U.S. and coalition soldiers in helping to overthrow a dictator who might also be described as having ruled with even worse "martial law, secret police, and torture chambers."

But Iraq would never do, as President Obama had already stated time and again (including in Egypt) that our involvement there was wrong.

And what of Israel, a full-blown democracy in the Middle East with even deeper ties to the United States than any Muslim-majority nation, one that has suffered more antidemocratic enemies than any other Middle East nation? Thus far, President Obama has traveled to Israel, our oldest and strongest ally in the Middle East, all of *no* times.[4] In itself that speaks volumes, not only to Israel, but to the rest of the world as well. This is to say nothing of the president's appeasement toward Iran, which we shall treat at length shortly.

Lest we get ahead of ourselves, this first-year tour by President Obama was not the only set of signals sent about our seriousness, or lack thereof, to the commitment of the war we were in, a war of ideas being only second to the physical war taking place on the battlefields of Iraq, Afghanistan, and, increasingly as we shall see, a war of ideas raging feverishly in the United States.

SILENCE AND MISDIRECTION

While it began during President Bush's second term, the new rhetoric and thinking accelerated with deliberate and breakneck speed in 2009 with the "outreach" to Arabic television, Turkey, Saudi Arabia, and Egypt. And here at home things were racing toward trouble just as quickly.

In her first testimony before Congress in February of 2009, Homeland Security secretary Janet Napolitano used the words *terror* and *terrorism* not once in her prepared opening remarks. By comparison, the department's first two secretaries, Tom Ridge and Michael Chertoff, used *terrorism* eleven and seven times, respectively, in theirs.[5] Remember, the agency's stated and official "overriding and urgent mission is to lead the unified national effort to secure the country and preserve our freedoms."[6] But from what?

Later, discussing her vocabulary with the German magazine *Der Spiegel*, Napolitano said, "[A]lthough I did not use the word 'terrorism,' I referred to 'man-caused' disasters. That is perhaps only a nuance, but it demonstrates that we want to move away from the politics of fear toward a policy of being prepared for all risks that can occur."[7] "Man-caused disasters," as in a human failure to prevent an oil rig explosion or a human setting off an alarm system by accident. Does the phrase *man-caused disasters* truly conjure up the concept of a planted bomb or an airplane hijacking? Or, does it sound more like a night watchman spilling his coffee over the motherboard of his computer terminal?

We are threatened by evil intention, and the administration's new focus removed both evil and intentionality—or at least heavily muted both.

This was not the only change we would see from the secretary of Homeland Security. In April 2009, Secretary Napolitano and Homeland Security issued a public report titled "Rightwing Extremism: Current Economic and Political Climate Fueling Resurgence in Radicalization and Recruitment."[8] Radical Islam and Middle Eastern– and Asian-based terrorism were not mentioned as threats to America, but "groups opposed to abortion and immigration" in America were, as were returning veterans in the U.S. armed services.[9] And they were labeled as potential organizers of "terrorist groups" or "lone wolf extremists."[10]

To his credit, even the Democratic chairman of the House Armed Services Committee criticized Secretary Napolitano for this report—not so much for not mentioning real terrorist threats (this was about the "right," mind you), but for the First Amendment implications in isolating pro-lifers, anti–illegal immigrant protestors, and American veterans as possible threats (and, mind you, without citing specific examples beyond conjecture and suspicion), as to why they would even see the need to issue the report.[11] Perhaps the secretary was thinking we should be grateful that at least the Department of Homeland Security had found a use for the word *terrorist.**

The silence and misdirection were not confined to the Department of Homeland Security, however. There seemed a government-wide anathematization of the term—and the thinking. In March 2009, for instance, an e-mail memo was sent to Department of Defense employees from the Office of Management and Budget, stating, "[T]his administration prefers to avoid using the term 'Long War' or 'Global War on Terror' [GWOT]. Please use 'Overseas Contingency Operation.'"[12] When this became public, the spokesman for the Office of Management and Budget denied this was an official directive but, rather, the work of some "career civil servant."[13] Nevertheless, as the *Washington Post* noted, "senior

---

* Given Nidal Hasan's attacks later in the year, one might think Napolitano and DHS were onto something. But two things correct this immediate assumption: (1) Hasan was not motivated by a pro-life or anti–illegal immigrant cause (or any other "right-wing" cause), and (2) he was not a returning veteran from a war front; indeed, he had never been deployed abroad and, as Mark Steyn would comment, if Hasan suffered from some form of traumatic stress syndrome, it may very well be the world's first example of "pre–traumatic stress syndrome," given his lack of serving on a war front.

administration officials had been publicly using the phrase 'overseas contingency operations' in a war context," among them the director of the Office of Management and Budget, Peter Orszag, and an assistant secretary of the air force.[14]

Contingency operations? But all this was only the beginning, of course. There was more to come.

WILLFUL IGNORANCE AND DENIALS

In November 2009, the day after the Fort Hood massacre, the president spoke from the White House, warning the American people about haste in assessing what had happened. "I would caution against jumping to conclusions until we have all the facts," the president intoned.[15] Of course, haste is relative. By then we already knew the assailant's name and a good deal of his biography, with Google page after Google page telling us almost all we needed to know about Hasan, including his religion, background, and, importantly, what he was shouting as he was shooting.

Back to the president's statement. Is it actually comforting or calming for us to be distracted from our enemy, or does it give us a lack of confidence from on high just when we need it most, and when our enemies are listening as well?

There was more terrorism in America at the end of 2009. On Christmas Day, Northwest Flight 253 headed into Detroit from the Netherlands as Umar Farouk Abdulmutallab, a Nigerian Muslim, tried to explode a bomb he carried aboard.[16] Abdulmutallab was thankfully stopped by an alert Dutch passenger, Jasper Schuringa, who pounced on Abdulmutallab as he was on fire, struggling to detonate his bomb.[17] It was not the elaborate apparatus of

Homeland Security, but, rather, a young Dutchman that saved the day, again.

We would soon learn that Abdulmutallab was tied to both al-Qaeda and Anwar al-Awlaki, Nidal Hasan's e-mail correspondent.[18] Indeed, we would learn from Abdulmutallab that al-Awlaki had instructed him to attempt his attack. More shocking still, the United States had knowledge of Abdulmutallab before Christmas 2009; at least some in our government did. Abdulmutallab's moderate and concerned father told the CIA about his son's radicalism the month before, and the CIA placed his name on a terrorist watch list.[19] Almost tragically, his name was never added to the "no-fly" list of the Transportation Safety Administration.[20]

Amazingly, it took the president three days to make a public statement about this near-spectacular attack, but the delay is not as important as what he did say when he finally spoke.

"This incident, like several that have preceded it," said the president, "demonstrates that an alert and courageous citizenry are far more resilient than an isolated extremist."[21] An "isolated extremist," not a terrorist. And don't lose that adjective, "isolated." The al-Qaeda and al-Awlaki ties would emerge quickly enough, but the first reaction—and one verbalized before enough was known—was to assume and to instruct that Abdulmutallab was working alone.

As if this were not quite enough, Secretary Napolitano's first comments about this attack on the Sunday news shows were, incredibly, "The system worked" and "Everything happened that should have."[22] The "system" that worked was a single good-willed and brave civilian passenger from the Netherlands. The rest of the "system" let a known radical board a plane with a bomb.

Incompetence, disregard, dismissal, and appeasement marked

this situation from beginning to end. We use *appeasement* deliberately. The administration's rhetoric ratcheted down evil and terrorism, ignoring its fuel and cause.

Official actions and announcements—such as presidential directives to shut down Guantánamo, the attempt to try high-value detainees like Khalid Sheikh Mohammed in civilian courts, investigating and possibly prosecuting CIA and DOJ officials from the Bush administration who authorized and practiced "enhanced interrogation techniques" against hardened terrorists, labeling such techniques "torture," and apologizing for such sins as "torture" before the international community—all served to telegraph pacification, not vigorous prosecution of a war.

Finally, recall Barack Obama's statement that terrorism grows out of "poverty and ignorance, helplessness and despair." Abdulmutallab, for the record, was raised with "[w]ealth, privilege and education."[23] But we already knew this view was pure rot. Osama bin Laden was born a millionaire, and Yasser Arafat died one. Ayman al-Zawahiri is a physician. Anwar al-Awlaki is the son of a successful academic. And Nidal Hasan was an American-born and trained physician and officer in the army. We could cite more examples, but this brief list should suffice to make the point about the economic privation of some of the most prominent abusers of civilization.

THE DANGER OF DAYDREAMS

Words like *appeasement* (and one could add *self-flagellation* and *denial* and *anxious propitiation* here as well) are admittedly pejorative. That's the point. The scope of history reveals that appeasement of tyrants and enemies fails those who employ the tactic. It is no different in this case. Just before the Christmas Day attempt, the RAND Corporation published a study on domestic terrorism and concluded that 2009, Obama's first year in office, "saw an unprecedented surge in terrorism events on U.S. soil."[24] The lead reporter noted that "there have been 32 terrorism-related events on these shores since 9/11 and that 12 of them occurred in 2009."[25*] That, again, was before Abdulmutallab's fiery lump of coal, and 2009 already had more events than any single year since 2001.[26**]

Given this, one would presume we would begin taking the terrorists as seriously as they were taking us. Perhaps the new direction was the wrong way, after all. Alas, as of this writing, there is no change in policy, and no change in the hearts and minds of our enemy.

In May 2010 Faisal Shahzad, a son of wealth from Pakistan, planted a bomb in Times Square. In testimony before Congress on the treatment of Shahzad, U.S. attorney general Eric Holder refused to use the words *radical Islam*—even as they were offered to him by Congressman Lamar Smith of the House Judiciary Committee—to describe the motivations of Shahzad and other terrorists. The transcript, as one journalist pointed out, nearly reads like a *Saturday Night Live* skit:

Smith: Let me go to my next question . . . in the case of all

---

* Such plots included an effort to blow up a train in Penn Station, New York; a gun attack on a military recruitment center in Little Rock, Arkansas; an effort to blow up a federal building in Springfield, Illinois; and more.

** And according to one analysis by our own State Department, there were more than 5,000 radical Islamic terrorist attacks worldwide in 2009 (see http://www.state.gov/s/ct/rls/crt/2009/140902.htm).

three attempts in the last year, the terrorist attempts, one of which was successful, those individuals have had ties to radical Islam. Do you feel that these individuals might have been incited to take the actions that they did because of radical Islam?

Holder: Because of?

Smith: Radical Islam.

Holder: There are a variety of reasons why I think people have taken these actions. It's—one, I think you have to look at each individual case. I mean, we are in the process now of talking to Mr. Shahzad to try to understand what it is that drove him to take the action.

Smith: Yes, but radical Islam could have been one of the reasons?

Holder: There are a variety of reasons why people . . .

Smith: But was radical Islam one of them?

Holder: There are a variety of reasons why people do things. Some of them are potentially religious . . .

Smith: Okay. But all I'm asking is if you think among those variety of reasons radical Islam might have been one of the reasons that the individuals took the steps that they did.

Holder: You see, you say radical Islam. I mean, I think those people who espouse a—a version of Islam that is not . . .

Smith: Are you uncomfortable attributing any other actions to radical Islam? It sounds like it.

Holder: No, I don't want to say anything negative about a religion that is not . . .

Smith: No, no. I'm not talking about religion. I'm talking about radical Islam. I'm not talking about the general religion.

Holder: Right. And I'm saying that a person, like Anwar Awlaki, for instance, who has a version of Islam that is not consistent with the teachings of it . . .

Smith: But . . .

Holder: . . . and who espouses a radical version . . .

Smith: But then is—could radical Islam have motivated these individuals to take the steps that they did?

Holder: I certainly think that it's possible that people who espouse a radical version of Islam have had an ability to have an impact on people like Mr. Shahzad.

Smith: Okay. And could it have been the case in one of these three instances?

Holder: Could that have been the case?

Smith: Yes, could—again, could one of these three individuals have been incited by radical Islam? Apparently, you feel that they could've been.

Holder: Well, I think potentially incited by people who have a view of Islam that is inconsistent with . . .

Smith: Okay. Mr. A. G., it's hard to get an answer yes or no, but let me go on to my next question.[27]

The first reaction from the attorney general is to deny "radical Islam" as an inspiration or motive for terrorism and say, repeatedly, the causes and motivations could be "a variety of reasons." And finally, after intense and further repeated questioning, the most we could get from our attorney general was that "it's possible that people who espouse a radical version of Islam have had an ability to have an impact on people like Mr. Shahzad." Possible.

People. Espouse. An ability. An impact. On people like. This is nothing shy of weakness, diversion, and dreaming.

NAMING AND CLAIMING

The curious thing about the administration's evasiveness here is its selectivity. Witness the blunt and backward words of our nation's chief counterterrorism official, Deputy National Security Advisor for Homeland Security and Counterterrorism John Brennan. At a speech he gave in May 2010 he affirmed *jihad* (a term most people, including most Muslims, translate as "holy war") as a "legitimate tenet of Islam," and went on to argue that the term *jihadists* should not be used to "describe America's enemies."[28] Said Brennan:

> Our enemy is not "terror" because terror is a state of mind and as Americans we refuse to live in fear. Nor do we describe our enemy as "jihadists" or "Islamists" because jihad is a holy struggle, a legitimate tenet of Islam, meaning to purify oneself or one's community, and there is nothing holy or legitimate or Islamic about murdering innocent men, women and children.
>
> Indeed, characterizing our adversaries this way would actually be counterproductive.[29]

The administration proudly posted the speech on the White House Web site. We will later delve deeper into the concept of *jihad* and the term *Islamist*, but suffice it to say for now that when Osama bin Laden intones to his followers to "join the jihad against them

[as] your duty," as he routinely does, be it to the battlefields of Iraq or Afghanistan or elsewhere, he is not asking his followers to purify themselves by holy and legitimate means—at least not means we would consider holy and legitimate. When Yasser Arafat spoke of a "jihad to liberate Jerusalem," it was not an appeal to silent meditation.[30] Nor when the Hamas charter states, "There is no solution for the Palestinian question except through Jihad," is it speaking of self-purification or morning ablutions, unless such purification includes a suicide mission, taking as many innocent lives as possible.[31]

As for not speaking of our enemy as *Islamists*, Bernard Lewis put the offense that some feel in context: "Understandably, Muslims complain when the media speak of terrorist movements and actions as 'Islamic' and ask why the media do not similarly identify Irish and Basque terrorists as 'Christian.' The answer is simple and obvious—they do not describe themselves as such. The Muslim complaint is understandable, but it should be addressed to those who make the news, not to those who report it."[32]

If using the term *Islam* or its variants, as with using the term *jihad*, is upsetting to anyone in describing the terrorism and violence committed in its name, it is the duty of nonviolent Muslims to tell their brethren so, not the duty of the victims or observers of such terror and violence to disbelieve those who commit terror and violence in their religion's name. A reporter, a victim, an astute observer can only be blamed for so much, and taking his enemy at his word is not a blameworthy event, not with a long trail of evidence alongside it. The same goes for a country targeted by those who say they are waging jihad against it in the name of their religion.

And a country's leadership that cannot muster the verbal

wherewithal to identify its enemy by taking its enemy seriously at its word—when the enemy tells us again and again what it is, who it is, what it will do, and then does it—is a country that has halfway surrendered to its enemy.

That surrender comes, dangerously, as one of the world's foremost incubators of terror-driven Islam is on the rise—Iran.

6

THE IRANIAN THREAT

G iven the current trajectory, Iran will become a nuclear power on the watch of President Barack Obama. Once a country goes nuclear (think Pakistan; think North Korea) the options for confronting it become very limited. With a country such as Iran, a country at war with us for more than thirty years, a country that has sponsored terrorist groups that have killed Americans en masse, a country whose leadership has spoken of the liquidation of Israel and openly questioned what a world without America would look like, it is impossible to conclude Iran would resist using its newly—and long desired—nuclear arsenal against us or an ally.

If we have arrived at this point where the government of the United States cannot speak about terrorism, barely a decade, ten years, after the greatest terrorist attack against this country (indeed, the worst terrorist attack the world has ever seen), and less than two years after the second-greatest terrorist attack against this country since 2001, we should not be surprised that the leading terrorist state in the world—Iran—would be coddled and appeased and its brutality ignored, even as it has made its desires for our death known and has acted on those desires wherever it can.

Barack Obama ran for office with promises of hope and change. Change we got, but not much hope, especially where Iran is concerned.

OBAMA'S NEW DIRECTION

In the debates leading up to the 2008 election, then U.S. senator Barack Obama told us exactly what he believed about Iran. Since that time, since his election, he has not only proven his sincerity; he has also made things dramatically worse.

During a candidate debate in 2007, then Senator Barack Obama said something very telling. When asked if he would meet with the leaders of such countries as Iran, Cuba, and Venezuela "without preconditions," he said, "I would. And the reason is this: that the notion that somehow not talking to countries is punishment to them—which has been the guiding diplomatic principle of this administration—is ridiculous."[1]

When later asked about this new approach to foreign policy, then Senator Obama justified his position, saying, "Strong countries and strong [p]residents talk to their adversaries. That's what Kennedy did with Khrushchev. That's what Reagan did with Gorbachev. That's what Nixon did with Mao."[2]

In that answer, Senator Obama betrayed a woeful ignorance of history. Ronald Reagan met no Soviet leaders during the entirety of his first term in office, not ever with Brezhnev, not ever with

Andropov, not ever with Chernenko. He met only with Gorbachev, and then only after he was assured Gorbachev was a different kind of Soviet leader—after Perestroika, not before. One illustrative moment of this came in 1983, when Secretary of State George Shultz was testifying before the Senate Foreign Relations Committee and Senator Paul Tsongas of Massachusetts asked him if President Reagan and the administration were not embarrassed that this may turn out to be the only administration in recent years not to have reached an arms control pact with Moscow. "So be it," is all that was said by Shultz.[3]

If Barack Obama wanted to affiliate with Richard Nixon, that was certainly his call. We doubt he embraced all of Richard Nixon's foreign- and defense-policy positions in Asia. And we also question whether Nixon's approach to China was as worthy of exultation as many think. Aside from liberalized economic trade that has enriched some Americans and some Chinese, has China proven itself less threatening than it used to be toward us? Was Taiwan's expulsion from the UN worth "Nixon to China"? That was, after all, China's price of admission.

As for the 1961 Kennedy-Khrushchev summit in Vienna, Kennedy himself admitted that Khrushchev "beat the hell out of me." Everyone agreed. Following Obama's comment, the *New York Times* was quick to remind that the then assistant secretary of defense, Paul Nitze, declared the meeting "a disaster"; one of Khrushchev's aides deemed Kennedy "very inexperienced, even immature"; and Khrushchev said the president was "too intelligent and too weak."[4] By any accurate reading of history, this summit went poorly for the United States and her allies.

And it got worse. Within two years of the summit, the Berlin Wall was up and the Cuban Missile Crisis had commenced. This hardly seems like the model for engagement with enemies, or in this case the leadership of Iran, but in either ignorance or defiance of history, it is the model that the president said he would prefer and employ.

THE RISE AND RULE OF THE MULLAHS

Iran was not always an enemy of the United States. Indeed, it was, under the Shah (imperfect as he was, autocratic though he was), a close ally. Under the Shah's rule one even witnessed relations with Israel. The Shah was not, however, powerful enough to prevent an Islamic uprising against his leadership in 1979, and most of us can still remember the 444-day crisis when the new regime took over the country and held fifty-two American hostages.

There are a great many descriptions of what took place when the Ayatollah Khomeini took over Iran, the most eloquent of which flows from the pen of Christopher Hitchens (no particular fan of the Shah's): "At the moment when Iran stood at the threshold of modernity, a black winged ghoul came flapping back from exile on a French jet and imposed a version of his own dark and heavy uniform on a people too long used to being bullied and ordered around."[5]

That dark and heavy uniform has smothered the country ever since. The intense brutality of Iran's ruling mullahs—the mullocracy—is one that famously put a price on a novelist's head* but, moreover and more dramatically, has successfully imposed its cloak of terror on its own and other people for decades. Today,

---

* Salman Rushdie

more than thirty years after the Iranian revolution, Freedom House still rates the country with the second-worst scores available for civil and political liberties in the world.[6]

There are not enough pages here to catalogue all the restrictions and abuses. What follows is a mere, bitter sampling:

- Islamic law—*Sharia*—provides the backbone of the penal code and breaks many of its citizens', permitting and encouraging "flogging, amputation, and execution by stoning or hanging for a range of social and political offenses."

- Speech is restricted and, when opposed to the state, curtailed and violently punished. Radio and television broadcasts are state controlled, and satellite dishes are basically outlawed. All books, whether domestically published or imported from abroad, are vetted by the "Ministry of Culture" to prevent wayward opinions and reporting.

- Freedom of assembly is prohibited to prevent dissident groups, and thousands of home raids are conducted by militia details to find and stop offenders.

- During the 2009 elections, protests and demonstrations were squelched by security forces who were later, reported Freedom House, "accused of raping and torturing detained demonstrators and opposition supporters, many of whom were subjected to televised show trials."

- Since President Mahmoud Ahmadinejad's 2005 ascension, the execution rate, including child executions, has rocketed almost 300 percent, and that's to say nothing of the dissidents and opposition workers who simply go "missing."[7]

How a regime treats its children in war—does it protect them, or use them?—is a good test for the regime's legitimacy and designs. During Iran's war against Iraq in the 1980s, the mullocracy showed us its view of life, children's life, by sending out preteens and teenagers to sweep minefields in advance of the Revolutionary Guard. They had no particular training or military equipment. The mines would be discovered as bits of the child scattered to the four winds. Sensitive to the likelihood of death, the mullahs provided each child with little plastic toy keys that promised to unlock paradise after the bombs detonated. Waves of children were so employed, marching into enemy fire while mines blew beneath their feet. Khomeini ordered half a million of the keys to supply the little martyrs.[8]

These child minesweepers were part of, were members of, the Basiji movement. This is the Iranian movement that President Ahmadinejad praises and whose official scarf he wears in public.

At this point, it is worth considering what Iran analyst Michael Ledeen has observed: "If you want to know what they will do to us, look at what they do to their own people."

Iran abroad is no better than Iran at home. It has been and is a financier of terror groups, including Hamas, Islamic Jihad, and Hezbollah—the same Hezbollah that has been targeting Americans and America's allies since 1983, in bombings, hijackings, and shootings everywhere from Beirut to Saudi Arabia to Argentina. And, there are now serious concerns that Hezbollah is operating in Venezuela.[9] Iran has also entered the battlefield against us in Iraq. Members of the Iranian Revolutionary Guard have invaded Iraq to fight us and our allies there, and military leaders have shown displays of recovered rocket-propelled grenades and one of "the most feared weapons faced by American and Iraqi troops" (a "canister designed to explode and spit out a molten ball of copper that cuts through armor") made in and smuggled from Iran.[10]

And we have yet to discuss Iran's nuclear ambitions.

THE PROSPECT OF WAR

The International Atomic Energy Agency had for years given Iran the benefit of the doubt about its uranium enrichment program, but after years of Iran's concealing both the number of its reactors and the advancement that had taken place in them, the IAEA was finally forced to conclude in early 2010 that it had found evidence that Iran's enrichment activities were not solely for peaceful purposes. The IAEA finally concluded it was "worried" Iran was "working on making a nuclear warhead."[11] The year before, it was discovered Iran had tested a neutron initiator, "the component that triggers a nuclear weapon. A neutron initiator has no peaceful application."[12]

Several books and papers have been written on Iran's nuclear intentions, so here is the summary as to what is currently known, as detailed by Middle East analyst James Phillips:

Iran has built an extensive and expensive nuclear infrastructure that is much larger than what would be necessary to support a civilian nuclear power program.

Iran sought to buy technology from A. Q. Khan's nuclear weapon proliferation network, which also provided assistance to Libya and North Korea.

Iran continues to conceal and lie about its nuclear weapons efforts.

Iran rejected a nuclear deal [in 2009] that would have advanced its civilian nuclear efforts, belying its claims that civilian purposes are its only motivation.[13]

What is uncertain is just how close Iran may be to actually building a nuclear weapon. Estimates going back to 2005 suggested Iran was about ten years away from such a capability, but those estimates have rapidly collapsed with each successive year of dithering by the West and the concomitant efforts inside Iran. Thus, we are all now reassured by the Obama administration that Iran, as of August 2010, was about 365 days away from such a weapon.[14] Here is the *New York Times* report from August 20, 2010:

> "We think that they have roughly a year dash time," said Gary Samore, President Obama's top adviser on nuclear issues, referring to how long it would take the Iranians to convert nuclear material into a working weapon. "A year is a very long period of time."[15]

"Roughly a year," which is "a very long period of time." That is the belief and posture of the administration as of this writing.

Despite all this—the terrorism, the flouting of inspections, the human rights depredations, and the secretive evasions of nonproliferation treaties—the disposition of the candidate was unpreconditioned negotiations. What has been the disposition of the candidate-cum-president?

No one wants a war with Iran any more than anyone wanted a war with the Soviet Union. And yet what ushered in the end of the Soviet Union was not dithering, was not appeasement, was not détente, was not negotiation, but rather, a loud voice of denunciation from the West, a voice calling the Soviet Union out for what it was, showing its leadership that we knew what it truly stood for, and that we would not be hoodwinked by it or ignore its vicious designs on the world any longer. Tied to these rhetorical efforts was vocal and financial support for the dissidents fighting against the Soviet Union and its umbrella dictatorships in other Eastern European states. And, sending a further signal to the leadership of our enemy, we began a massive military buildup at home.

That record, *that history lesson,* has been completely ignored and reversed by today's American policies. It is a history lesson that should have been heeded. Instead, the opposite tack has been taken, with praise not for the reformers and dissidents in Iran but for the leadership. To the reformers and dissidents, we have offered a cold hand and a deaf ear.

Where once, in 1979, the Iranian people may have had cause to support the Islamic revolution in Iran, they have now grown tired and weary of its brutalizing theocratic rule and repression. And, seeking help to give a shove to their rulers, they looked to what their leaders called the "Great Satan," America. Help has not been coming.

Taking a page from how we did offer assistance in the 1980s to those under the Soviets and their satellite states, Michael Ledeen offered a nonviolent path as to how we might help such an effort today. Testifying to the Senate in 2006, Dr. Ledeen said:

> We should greatly expand our support for private radio and tele-
> vision broadcasters, both here and in Europe, and we need to get
> serious about using our own broadcasts as revolutionary instru-
> ments. We should not compete for market share, and we should
> not be in the entertainment business; we should be broadcasting

interviews with successful revolutionaries from other countries, as well as with the few Iranian dissidents who reach the
free world. We should also broadcast conversations with experts
on non-violent revolution. The Iranians need to learn, in detail,
what works and what does not. They need to see and hear the
experiences of their revolutionary comrades.

We must also provide them with the wherewithal for
two vitally important revolutionary actions: build resources
for a strike fund, and get them modern instruments of com-
munication. The strike fund speaks for itself: workers need to
be able to walk off the job, knowing they will be able to feed
their families for several weeks. The instruments of commu-
nication include servers, laptops, satellite and cell phones and
phone cards.[16]

Neither the Bush nor Obama administrations took these
ideas, although one called the Iranian regime out for what it was—
"evil"—and the other so far has not. Quite the opposite, in fact.*

IMMORAL EQUIVALENCE

On March 20, 2009 the president sent a videotaped message to the
people and the leadership of Iran on the occasion of the Persian
New Year. A message not to just the people, mind you, but to the
people *and the leadership.* "I would like to speak directly to the people and leaders of the Islamic Republic of Iran"—each on an equal

---

* While it is true President George Bush would call the Iranian regime "evil," it is
not true his administration refused to negotiate with it.

plane, as if sending a message to the people and leaders of Great Britain or France or Australia.[17]

He continued: "Indeed, you will be celebrating your New Year in much the same way that we Americans mark our holidays—by gathering with friends and family, exchanging gifts and stories, and looking to the future with a renewed sense of hope."[18] This assessment of Iran—that Iranians can celebrate the way Americans can—is far from the reality of what actually does or can take place in Iran. Free gatherings and a sense of hope are some of the last things Iranians have. To put on par what Iranians can do with what we can do is to either completely misunderstand Iran or to completely ignore the people's cry for human rights there.

President Obama concluded his message by saying, "With the coming of a new season, we're reminded of this precious humanity that we all share."[19] The shared humanity of stonings? Of punitive amputations? Mass arrests? Child minesweepers? The president was not ignorant of widespread human rights violations in Iran, nor was he linking America with those actions. He was, simply, ignoring them. Conciliating. Whitewashing. Appeasing. This was the same approach the administration had undertaken domestically—refusing to call Islamic terrorism by its proper name here, whenever it belched forth its toxins against America. But in emboldening the leadership of Iran with such a message, he was doing something else quite damaging as well: telling the dissidents, our prospective future allies, that we will ignore them and their plight at almost any cost and for almost any deal.

A lesson here is instructive. When President Ronald Reagan spoke of the Soviet Union as the evil empire and was criticized by the international foreign policy establishment for saying such words, two big and important things happened: (1) the Soviet Union became no more aggressive than it already had been, and (2) the dissidents in the Soviet Union were, for the first time in years, emboldened and given hope. Here is how former–Soviet prisoner Natan Sharansky put it in an interview some years later when asked what it meant to him and his fellow prisoners when President Reagan so labeled the Soviet Union:

> There was a long list of all the Western leaders who had lined up to condemn the evil Reagan for daring to call the great Soviet Union an evil empire right next to the front-page story about this dangerous, terrible man who wanted to take the world back to the dark days of the Cold War. This was the moment. It was the brightest, most glorious day. Finally a spade had been called a spade. Finally, Orwell's Newspeak was dead. President Reagan had from that moment made it impossible for anyone in the West to continue closing their eyes to the real nature of the Soviet Union.
>
> It was one of the most important, freedom-affirming declarations, and we all instantly knew it. For us, that was the moment that really marked the end for them, and the beginning for us. The lie had been exposed and could never, ever be untold now.[20]

A far cry different from putting the prisoners and the leadership in the same moral position, a far cry different from speaking of the Soviet leaders and the Americans' shared commitment to humanity. "Confusion," wrote Nobel Laureate Elie Wiesel, is "when good and evil are put on the same plane and the wicked receive the countenance of the just."[21]

A HOPE STOLEN, A CHANCE SQUANDERED

Perhaps successive United States governments can someday be forgiven for not doing more for the people of Iran up to the summer of 2009. But in June 2009 an election for the presidency of Iran was held. It was internationally condemned as a farcical election even before it took place, but something new took place after the victor, President Mahmoud Ahmadinejad, was announced.

Mass protests filled the streets—followed by an equally mass crackdown and brutalization of those protestors. Before the ultimate crackdown, there was a brief shining moment when, along with the opposition in Iran, people around the Western world wore green lapel flags in sympathetic support with the Iranian opposition leaders and protestors risking their lives on the streets there.

And we helped kill it. As one observer on the ground in Iran put it in the *New York Times*, "Some protesters I met on the streets of Tehran pointedly asked me, 'Where's Obama?'"[22]

Here is the answer: When asked what message he would give to the Iranian leaders and protestors, President Barack Obama uttered what would perhaps be his most famous or infamous words of the first year of his presidency: "It is not productive, given the history of US-Iranian relations to be seen as meddling—the US president, meddling in Iranian elections."[23] In reiterating why he would not meddle, he said, "The United States respects the sovereignty of the Islamic Republic of Iran."[24]

And there was the shot, the shock, heard round the world and, especially, on the streets of Tehran: the United States would take no position, would neither side with the mullocracy nor the dissidents being crushed on the streets. Of course, anytime one stakes a claim of neutrality as between tyrants with guns and civilians without them, it is not a true claim of neutrality; it is, rather, a staking of a claim with the interests of the stronger.

Organic protests of reform rise up too infrequently in tyrannies. Someone needed to show those students and those protesters that someone was on their side, that someone actually cared about them. It may have been our only chance for nonviolent regime change. And we sat on it. Our administration's talk of continuing to press for open dialogue with the leaders of Iran was not anything close to appropriate then. But that is exactly what our administration continued to do.

As Vaclav Havel (someone who knew what it was like to live under oppression) said at the time, "Expressions of solidarity with those who are defending human rights, with students and others, are important."[25] To reassert respect—that's the word the president used, *respect*—for Iran's sovereignty at a time of a stolen and fraudulent election, with brutality on the streets being committed against those demonstrating against the fraudulent election, in a regime that is the lead sponsor of terror in the Middle East, that thwarts weapons inspections as it attempts to nuclearize itself, that has been at war with us for more than three decades, and that speaks of a world without Israel or America—well, respect for its sovereignty (never mind not meddling) is the last thing the United States should have been standing for.

The United States can stand with democratic reformers or with brutal thugs in any given country. It can give hope or take it. It cannot do both. To paraphrase John F. Kennedy: in times of great moral crisis, we should not maintain our neutrality.

Diplomacy is one thing; freedom is another—and for all of us who have wanted nonmilitary inspired freedom to take root in Iran, that moment was upon us and we slammed the door on it.

June 2009 was Iran's Tiananmen Square, the only difference being that in Tiananmen there was no realistic hope of the Chinese regime collapsing. This made our government's reaction in 2009 even worse than Tiananmen, which was, itself, bad. We had the moment, and we squandered it. Iran had its moment, and it was lost—by an American president who had boasted of his skills at community organizing and defending the oppressed.

Admittedly, we seem to have been caught flat-footed and unable to recognize what was starting in Iran in the aftermath of the elections. Our on-the-ground intelligence in Iran has been poor for a very long time, though bloggers and analysts here and abroad had been citing the revolutionary hopes and dreams of Iranian students for a very long time, Michael Ledeen among them. Nevertheless, we should not have been fully surprised by the administration's Stephen A. Douglas "don't care" attitude that did come in the wake of the elections in Iran. Consider the administration's appreciation for our own nation's popular uprising; as the *New York Times* reported just two weeks prior to the Iranian plebiscite:

> [T]he State Department sent a cable to its embassies and consulates around the world notifying them that "they may invite representatives from the government of Iran" to their Independence Day celebrations—annual receptions that typically feature hot dogs, red-white-and-blue bunting and some perfunctory remarks about the founding fathers.
>
> Administration officials characterized the move as another in a series of American overtures to Iran.[26]*

---

* Ultimately, after much public criticism, the administration canceled these invitations, with Secretary of State Hillary Clinton, saying, "Unfortunately, circumstances have changed." What exactly changed between the invites—or

THE AMBASSADOR OF DEATH

If the use of the word *appeasement* has been too shocking for readers up until this point, perhaps we have now sufficiently defined it and given it adequate context.

Iran edges closer to nuclear weaponization by the day; it is "roughly a year" from that point. And lest we think more diplomacy is the answer, Iran announced in 2010 that it intends to start construction on ten new uranium enrichment sites in 2011.[27] This, after four sets of UN-passed sanctions; this, after a very great deal of diplomatic speak from the United States about "respect" for the sovereignty of Iran (or the "Islamic Republic of Iran," as President Obama prefers to speak of it); this, after promises and offers of negotiation; this, after promising not to meddle in the affairs of Iran.

On the other side of the leadership equation, President Ahmadinejad has not ceased arming for war and destruction. Force is the kind of diplomacy he understands and uses. Announcing Iran's first domestically built unmanned bomber aircraft in 2010, Ahmadinejad labeled it "the ambassador of death."[28]

When the history books are written about what was and was not done while the world's worst terrorist state was building the world's worst weapon and terrorizing its own and others, we would like those books to mention there were those like Michael Ledeen and Jay Nordlinger and Michael Rubin and Brian Kennedy and Bret Stephens and a handful of others who understood all this and did their best to publicize it. Should such horrors come to pass, our guess is the first book on the event will be entitled *While*

1979—and the cancelation is hard to divine.

America Slept. It belongs to all of us to keep that book from being written.

Such prevention requires that we understand that the leadership in Iran—from the mullahs to the president—is not a leadership of reasonable, moral, or even sane actors. The regime does not believe in a military race it can survive. Rather, it believes in a death cult whereby the death and destruction of others, attended by its own martyrdom if necessary, is the way to vindicate Allah. As Bernard Lewis has pointed out, for the current leadership of Iran, "death is not a deterrent, it is an inducement."[29] Diplomacy simply will not deter it—regime change is, or was, the only answer.

For the leadership of America to ignore what *has* taken place in Iran, what *is* taking place in Iran, what Iran *is* exporting, all the while seeking more negotiations along the way, is but part and parcel of how the administration has treated Islamic terrorism here at home: refusing to call it by its proper name, refusing to see it for what it is.

The sad and dangerous irony here is that once upon a time we needed covert intelligence to help discover the nature of our enemies' intentions. That was then. Now they tell us openly, loudly, time and time again. Yet we ignore them. This is a betrayal of more than moral clarity; it is a betrayal of reality. And reality can be a merciless avenger when betrayed.

7

FALSE PEACE
AND TRUE PEACE

As President Bush before him, President Obama speaks of Islam as "a religion of peace." The difference is that the Bush administration had no trouble in also linking Islam to terrorism, insisting rogue adherents had hijacked the faith. The term *radical Islam* was employed to distinguish it from mainstream belief. But the Obama administration displays a shocking level of foolishness or knavery by downgrading and downplaying the connection between Islam and terrorism— or even, as we've seen, admitting the *reality of terrorism*. Instead it validates expressions of the faith by, as we saw with counterterrorism advisor John Brennan, redefining words like *jihad* and ending up praising aspects of violence in Islam.

BOWING TO LIES

We say "foolishness" or "knavery" and want to provide one qualification. All of this may be in the service, the deliberate service, of
something else—appeasement. The thought seems to be that if we
speak nicely of Islam and ignore the terrorism it can produce, then
Islamists will respect us more or lay down their swords. Such an
understanding flies in the face of everything Islamists have told us;
they want our defeat, not a refurbished détente that comes from
soft language and retreat.

Aside from the geopolitical and domestic security problems
of speaking so kindly of Islam while excluding any recognition
of its terrorist elements, there is the political problem. Witness a
2010 poll from the Pew Research Center that revealed 18 percent
of the American population believed President Obama to actually
be a Muslim.[1]

There are any number of explanations for this belief, but
in some respects it was actually odd that the number was so
low, given not only his name but also his very deliberate efforts
to speak of his "Muslim roots" as well as his manifold efforts
to speak up on behalf of Islam. One thinks of his 2009 trav-
els, bowing his head before the king of Saudi Arabia, and giving
speeches in Egypt and Turkey where he said things such as: "I
have known Islam on three continents before coming to the
region where it was first revealed. That experience guides my
conviction that partnership between America and Islam must
be based on what Islam is, not what it isn't. And I consider it part
of my responsibility as president of the United States to fight
against negative stereotypes of Islam wherever they appear."[2]
And this: "Americans have Muslims in their families or have

lived in a Muslim majority country. I know, because I am one of them."[3]

But it was his bowing to the king of Saudi Arabia in 2009 in London that revealed so very much.[4] The American president bowed shortly after apologizing for America on several fronts abroad and saying that America had been "arrogant" and "dismissive" to other countries in the past. And apologizing for imprisoning terrorists at such places as Guantánamo Bay. And after claiming America engaged in torture and, under him, would do so no longer. When he was not saying such things abroad, he was saying them in front of the United Nations.

The words were one thing, and bad enough, but the bowing was another. This was symbolism that not only denigrated America past and present but also sent a strong signal of obeisance—and to what? To a king of an Arab country whose human rights record is execrable and whose record of funding terrorist organizations is legend. Or, as in the case of the United Nations, to other countries' leaders who have blood on their hands and less than nothing to teach us, or any civilized people, about what human rights truly are. Let us not put too fine a point on it: it showed national humiliation.*

And what has any of that accomplished? Were there fewer terrorist attacks in America or against American personnel as a result? No, in fact, there were more. Bending over backward (and forward)

---

* Bowing to a foreign leader as a matter of policy is bad enough, but there is something uniquely unbefitting of it given the history of all at play in such a scene. One is actually put in mind of the story of Abraham Lincoln, traveling to Richmond, Virginia, in 1865 after Union forces had captured the city. Free black men kneeled in front of the president, who then told them, "Don't kneel to me. That is not right. You must kneel to God only and thank Him for the liberty you will hereafter enjoy" (David Herbert Donald's *Lincoln* [New York: Simon & Schuster, 1995], 576).

to speak so positively of Islam while whitewashing its violence has yielded no surrender of any kind from the enemy, no easing of tensions whatsoever. And it led to a false belief about the president himself.

Just how much whitewashing has gone on is hard to quantify, but in an article for the liberal *New Republic*, Reuel Marc Gerecht of the Foundation for the Defense of Democracies said that getting a straight answer on Islam from U.S. government officials is practically impossible: "Ask someone in the Obama administration about jihad, and unless the official knows the conversation is off the record—and sometimes even if it is off the record—that official likely will become a bit panicked, nonplussed, and try to change the subject." Conversations about Islam in Washington, D.C., he said, "have become boring, lightweight, and sometimes inane."[5]

Nobody is fooled, however. "Muslim militants aren't children," said Gerecht. "They know a hell of a lot more about their faith than do American presidents, who assert that 'Islam is a religion of peace.'"[6]

So let us get to it. What is Islam? Is it a religion of peace? And what are the policy implications and prescriptions to such an answer?

One can see the potential political savvy in saying, as President Bush did, that the United States was not at war with, nor would be going to war against, Islam. But the statement that Islam is a religion of peace, echoed again and again, as if it were a required utterance in both the Bush and Obama administrations, simply does not ring true without some very bold asterisks.

Better than foregoing assurances is reiterating how many times Americans have taken up arms to defend the liberty and security of Muslims—in Europe, in Africa, and in the Middle East. But "Islam is a religion of peace" became the mantra from our government and its leaders, and with that mantra came a feeling, an imprint, that perhaps our government did not fully understand the nature of the threat. And, at the same time, that we could let our guard down.

THE AMERICAN AGREEMENT

There is a basic thirst in America to treat all religions with respect and, at the same time, an ingrained distaste for openly discussing various religious theologies critically in polite society. This thirst and attendant distaste comes from our very beginnings and is enshrined in our Bill of Rights. There is no greater explication of the notion of religious freedom than that provided by our first president, George Washington, in his letter to the Touro Synagogue in Rhode Island in 1790. Washington penned:

> All possess alike liberty of conscience and immunities of citizenship.
>
> It is now no more that toleration is spoken of, as if it was by the indulgence of one class of people that another enjoyed the exercise of their inherent natural rights. For happily the Government of the United States, which gives to bigotry no sanction, to persecution no assistance, requires only that they who live under its protection, should demean themselves as good citizens, in giving it on all occasions their effectual support.[7]

President Washington concluded his letter, quoting from the fourth chapter of the book of the prophet Micah: "May the

Children of the Stock of Abraham, who dwell in this land, continue to merit and enjoy the good will of the other inhabitants; while every one shall sit under his own vine and fig tree, and there shall be none to make him afraid."[8]

The terms of this implied religious freedom contract were clear: Those who wished to practice their religion here were welcome and free, provided they also followed the laws of the land, remained peaceful, and gave "effectual support" to their country.

In our nonjudgmental modern temperament, we have nurtured the vine and fig trees, we have protected them, and we have built rhetorical and legal fences around them. But we have forgotten and deemphasized and cut down the obligations owed by the other party to this agreement—the expectation that those dwelling under those trees, that those who desire to live under our protection, would obey the laws and give this country their effectual support. That side of the contract is today unattended, if not altogether forgotten.

We should not be embarrassed or reticent to point out that no country has historically or presently granted more rights and freedoms to more religions and differing kinds of religious believers than the United States of America; the few historical caveats to religious practice here only serve to further illustrate this point (note, for example, the refusal to tolerate Mormon polygamy). Once such a religious community brought itself into compliance with neutral laws of general applicability here, once it reformed itself, it was simply left alone, with none to make it afraid.

Given its history it has become jarring, if not offensive, to constantly be told—lectured at—that Islam is a religion of peace. Have Americans treated Muslims in a way that requires such a lecture? Have there been outbreaks of violence against American Muslims beyond the odd nut-job perpetrator? Have we as a country, under both Republican and Democratic Party administrations, not shown a wide berth of tolerance and civil liberty that, for example, might be contradistinguished with how Franklin Roosevelt's administration and the American people treated Japanese Americans in World War II?

HARDLINERS AND MODERATES

This discussion came to the fore with the debate over the Ground Zero mosque in New York City. As already rehearsed, Americans were told both by the administration and the cultural elites that there was not only a First Amendment right for the Muslims to build a mosque there but that the mosque's leader, Imam Feisal Abdul Rauf, was the beau ideal of a "moderate Muslim."

The defense of Imam Rauf from the government and the cultural elites, much like the defense made of Tarik Ramadan, showed nothing if not desperation—a desperation to actually find moderacy in Islam. But, as Paul Berman has pointed out, it does a country no favor to define moderation down by labeling the immoderate moderate.

Looking at Rauf's statements, how could it be otherwise? Here was a man—pleading for tolerance and understanding and nothing more than the right to sit under his own vine and fig tree—who after 9/11 said the United States was an accessory to the event. Here was a man who could not bring himself to denounce Hamas as a terrorist organization. Here was a man who said, "The United States has more Muslim blood on its hands than al Qaida has on its hands of innocent non-Muslims."[9] Here was a man who praised Muslim Brotherhood cleric Yusuf al-Qaradawi (who, among other things, issued a fatwa, or religious ruling, permitting the kidnapping and slaying of Americans in Iraq and is barred from entry into the United States).[10] Going back to Washington's letter, these are the statements of a man offering effectual support for terrorism—not for the United States of America.

One does not have to be a hardliner to see that Rauf is not the kind of moderate so many wished he were. But what of other Muslims, the millions who have lived peaceably in America and other parts of the world, the Muslims so many of us have seen in our neighborhoods and markets, have known as acquaintances or even friends? This is the core of the question about moderate Islam.

There are analogues we can all comprehend about religious believers and their distancing and disagreement with the ortho-dox fundamentals or doctrines of their faith. There are a great many, a majority, of Jews, for example, who proudly claim they are Jewish but do not follow every commandment of Jewish ortho-doxy and teaching. And there are, equally, a majority of Catholics and people who call themselves Catholic who do not follow all of their church's doctrines—and there are both Jews and Catholics who will say certain of these teachings do not apply any longer, or do not apply to them, as they have their own beliefs and justifi-cations that render such orthodoxy and doctrine inapplicable or inappropriate for themselves while maintaining *some* or *enough* of their faith's teachings to still proudly call themselves adherents to the faith.

Two questions immediately arise: How can one compare Islam, with so many dictums about war, with Judaism and Catholicism, when Judaism and Catholicism do not preach or teach or justify violence? Or, alternatively, do not Judaism and Christianity also have their violent teachings and pasts?

CHRISTIAN AND JEWISH VIOLENCE

Let us take the second point first and immediately dismiss the argument now popular in some quarters that the Bible is more violent than the Koran.[11] In the history of Christianity, there certainly are violent episodes where Christian leaders have committed, instigated, and justified bloody war—against others and themselves, no doubt about this. But the New Testament itself is evidence to how such history and examples diverge and contradict the basic *doctrines* of Christianity. As Professor David Gelernter has pointed out, the New Testament is nearly a manifesto of pacifism, with emphases so common to our parlance that many people do not even realize their source, for example:

- "Judge not, that ye be not judged."
- "He that is without sin among you, let him first cast a stone."
- "Wherein thou judgest another, thou condemnest thyself."
- "Resist not evil."
- "Whoever shall smite thee on thy right cheek, turn to him the other also."
- "Blessed are the meek: for they shall inherit the earth."[12]

Put plainly, the highest and most revered person in all of Christianity was not a warrior; rather, Christ taught his followers to bless their accusers and pray for their abusers. He is popularly known by such appellations as "Prince of Peace" and "Lamb."

Let us not excuse Christian violence in the past or present, but let us underscore the difficulty in justifying acts of violence based on Christian morality as taught in the New Testament.* "Indeed," noted scholar Raymond Ibrahim, "it took centuries of theological debate, from Augustine to Aquinas, to rationalize defensive war—articulated as 'just war.'"[13] And, indeed, Christians in need of justifications for violence usually have to turn to the Old Testament, scriptures they adopted from Judaism.

It is this supposed textual font of violence that makes Judaism a different case when it comes to religions of violence. Wrote David Gelernter, "Jewish morality is warrior morality. It is no accident that Abraham, Moses, and David, the Bible's greatest heroes, should all have been described as warriors."[14]**

At a basic and rudimentary reading, there is a great deal of violence in the Old Testament, the Tanakh, as Jews know it. But the deeper questions involve what that violence is about and its applicability to the Jewish way of life and religious law today. The answers are a great deal more innocent than the rudimentary reading, and equally different from the violence found in Islam.

Let us start with this test: Can a reader of these words count on an entire hand the number of Jewish terrorists or criminals who have cited the Bible to justify their actions? Can a reader count on

---

* Two additional points need to be made here: None of this is to say Christians cannot engage in just wars and be true to their faith. It is to say that one has to work his way through the obvious and basic teachings of the New Testament to justify such engagement in said wars. Second, we are not unaware that there have been several instances of violence committed in Christianity's name, even recently (think of abortion clinic shootings or bombings, for example). But again, in those instances there seems a very high burden to find justification in the New Testament. Acts of violence committed in the name of Christ over the past several years have been roundly condemned by most Christian leaders of any repute.

** Note again the emerging intellectual trend in which professors of theology are wont to see the Bible as more violent than the Koran.

an entire hand the number of Jewish terrorists at all? Having, perhaps, come up with some examples, can one find those examples outside of one small patch of earth—Israel? And can one find an absence of denunciation and punishment from Israeli authorities and religious leaders for those acts? One cannot.

One can find a lot of blood in the Jewish scriptures, the book of Joshua, for one example. And one can find commandments that run counter to Western views of peace and love in later works as well, from the Talmud to the Shulchan Aruch (a fifteenth-century codification of Jewish law). But elites who wish to equate the Bible and the Koran misunderstand, ignore, or deny the difference between a historical account and a living injunction. The wars of the Old Testament, wrote British journalist and author Melanie Phillips, "are merely a historical record and its injunctions to smite the foes of the Jews are specific and confined to the participants in those historic events. There are *no* divine injunctions in the Hebrew Bible to kill unbelievers." She went on to note that "Judaism . . . has [never] sought to possess any lands beyond its own. It has no problem with other faiths, provided they leave it alone."[15] One may take note here that "political Judaism," as found in the self-described "Jewish state" of Israel, allows for non-Jews—including Muslims—to not only vote in elections but be elected to its parliament.

Phillips also noted that Judaism, almost alone among other faiths, "does not demand converts." Jews are instructed to *not* seek converts. Rabbis are, in fact, instructed to turn away would-be converts when they first approach. Much of this is based on a verse from Micah: "All the nations may walk in the name of their gods, but we will walk in the name of the LORD our God for ever and ever."[16]

By contrast the Koran instructs, "Fight those who do not

believe in Allah, nor in the latter day, nor do they prohibit what Allah and His Apostle have prohibited, nor follow the religion of truth, out of those who have been given the Book, until they pay the tax in acknowledgment of superiority and they are in a state of subjection."[17] Similarly, we find in the Hadith, "I have been commanded to fight against people so long as they do not declare that there is no god but Allah, and he who professed it was guaranteed the protection of his property and life on my behalf except for the right affairs rest with Allah."[18]

As for commands of seeming violence in the Talmud or Shulchan Aruch, the conditions within them, to engage in them, are so strict, so detailed, as to ensure their nullity. For example, take the death penalty itself. The rabbis of the Talmud discussing the imposition of the penalty ultimately conclude, "A Sanhedrin [Jewish court] that puts a man to death once in seven years is called destructive. Rabbi Eliezer ben Azariah says: even once in seventy years. Rabbi Akiba and Rabbi Tarfon say: had we been in the Sanhedrin none would ever have been put to death."[19]

In addition, Jews were commanded to set up "cities of refuge" for those who had committed manslaughter so they would be unharmed by vengeful family members. And where there may be a law (as in the Shulchan Aruch) to slay Jewish heretics, it is simply not applicable today, if it ever were. The rules surrounding that commandment are written so as to practically render it void.[20*] Any serious reading or experience of the tradition reveals a clear reluctance toward violence.

---

* For example, prior to killing the heretic, the rule is to talk him out of his heresy. If the heretic continues, it is ruled that the problem was in the person trying to talk him out of the heresy and that he was ineffective, making the problem not so much the heretic as his teacher.

This is, simply put, not so with the Koran and doctrinal Islam. Others have spent a good deal of time detailing the passages discussing the violence in the Koran and other Islamic doctrine. There is little need to run the litany of passages here. Suffice it to say that passages such as, "Slay the idolaters wherever ye find them, arrest them, besiege them, and lie in ambush everywhere for them" and "Prophet! Make war on the unbelievers and the hypocrites! . . . Hell shall be their home, an evil fate" speak for themselves.[21]

Thus, when professors such as Phillip Jenkins at Penn State argue that "the Islamic scriptures in the Quran were actually far less bloody and less violent than those in the Bible," and that "[b]y the standards of the time, which is the 7th century A.D., the laws of war that are laid down by the Quran are actually reasonably humane" and that "[t]here is a specific kind of warfare laid down in the Bible which we can only call genocide," they are, on the one hand, being too charitable to the teachings of Islam while, on the other hand, too dismissive of context to the teachings of Judaism and Christianity.[22]

Even admitting to the peacefulness of Jews and Christians compared to Muslims today, as Jenkins does, the blood and war described in the Old Testament are, again, not prescriptive but descriptive. It is worth noting that precisely because of the blood he spilled in waging wars, so revered a figure as King David was not allowed by God to build the first Temple. That honor went to "a man of peace"—his son Solomon.[23]

To argue for the relative pacifism of the Koran and the teachings of Islam by calling it a religion of peace or by pointing to equal or worse violence in the Bible is to both misunderstand the difference between "documenting a practice" and "commanding it" and to dismiss (at best) what practicing Orthodox Jews, fundamentalist

Christians, and doctrinal Islamists believe. Judaism may have a good deal of war in its history, and those stories of war may be met with countervailing regret, but too much of Islam teaches that its war and violence are still relevant and recommended.

UNDERSTANDING ISLAMIC VIOLENCE

At this point, given general distastes for hyperanalyzing another's religion, many will ask, "What does it matter if Islam is a religion of war or not?" This question is more than appropriate, in fact fitting, to the general American temperament, but the answer is one most Americans have reluctantly been forced to answer. As the exiled Iranian writer Amir Taheri argued in 2001:

> [I]t is impolite, not to say impolitic, to subject Islam to any criticism. Yet to claim that the attacks [of September 11] had nothing to do with Islam amounts to a whitewash. It is not only disingenuous but also a disservice to Muslims, who need to cast a critical glance at the way their faith is taught, lived, and practiced. Even worse, the refusal to subject Islam to rational analysis is a recipe for further fanaticism.[24]

We will get to the "critical glance" momentarily, but first, to the point that the September 11 attacks—and every prior and subsequent attack committed by Muslims in the name of Islam and Allah—had at least *something* to do with Islam is nearly impossible to ignore, and more important, not to forget or dismiss.

If we are at war (and it is worth remembering that war has been declared on us), it is the most vital of first steps to identify the enemy, to know who attacked. And when Muslim terrorists attack, they are both Muslims and terrorists. Even if many wish to say they are not true Muslims, or they are perverting or hijacking Islam, or that they are immoderate Muslims, the terrorists themselves tell us they are Muslims, and they cite Muslim theology to justify their attack—a theology too few Muslims seem willing or able to refute as doctrinally unsound.

Are these terrorists misguided or merely wrong by claiming justification in their religion, by claiming Islam as their cause, by claiming to act as good Muslims? Ask that question and things get difficult—or have been made difficult by politicians and scholars.

The first task of any scientist (political or otherwise) is to see things as they truly are. And while, to borrow again from Professor Bernard Lewis, it is dangerous to exaggerate, it is equally dangerous to ignore and neglect. Said Lewis, "Most Muslims are not fundamentalists, and most fundamentalists are not terrorists, but most present-day terrorists are Muslims and proudly identify themselves as such."[25] In seeing or hearing things as they really are, we cannot avoid noting that Muslim terrorists who commit acts of terror against us tell us they are acting in the name of their religion and of Allah. Should we take them seriously? Should we take their word for it? We risk our own demise if we do not.

As many scholars and writers have detailed, and as a serious lay reader will discover, there are several active commands to jihad and physical violence in the Koran, especially for such sins as idolatry and apostasy, but for lesser sins as well, including hypocrisy and adultery.[26] It would be easy to say, and it is tempting to say, this is Islamic orthodoxy and "moderate Muslims" do not believe that these are valid and binding. The moment this point is stipulated, however, the next question arises: What is a "moderate Muslim"? For a variety of baffling but legitimate reasons, it is hard to say.

ISLAMIC AMBIVALENCE

So what do we do with the statement that Islam is a religion of peace? The best wisdom we can find and accept is this: for those Muslims who wish to practice their faith in peace (with each other and with the society around them), they surely have interpreted their religion as one of peace.

Many of us know such Muslims and cannot imagine their participation in terrorist endeavors, though we may hesitate in asking too many questions or probing too deeply. For them, and to them, Islam is a religion of peace. They sit under their own vine and fig tree, even if we may have worries about their commitment to their effectual support of their country—worries raised by the kinds of things said on behalf of their religion by so-called moderate clerics and mainstream Muslim civil rights organizations.

Another class of Muslims, such as Dr. Zuhdi Jasser of the American Islamic Forum for Democracy, invite questions and dialogue. They are happy to talk about Islam and what they believe about America, the war, terrorism. But Dr. Jasser will also readily admit Islam needs reform. He will tell you, to him, Islam is about prayer, fasting, and acting with good moral character, about which there is plenty in the Koran and Hadiths to instruct. As for the violent precepts and teachings, Dr. Jasser (a former officer in the U.S. Navy) has no patience or tolerance and will say they need to be reinterpreted for the modern era. Of Dr. Jasser and likeminded practitioners of Islam, there is no question as to what is or can be meant by Islam being a religion of peace, and there is no question as to the effectual support of this country. Islam *can* satisfy the George Washington test *if it is reformed.*

But there are too few Muslims like Dr. Jasser who are willing to speak out the way he has, who are willing to agree that the medieval must change and conform to the modern, that there needs to be not mere recognition, but celebration of a society like ours that allows Muslims not only to practice their faith freely, but also to speak about anything else as well—complete with a reliance on the security and the laws of this country.

The reason so many people do not accept the notion that Islam is a religion of peace is that for every Dr. Jasser there are several more Imam Raufs. The latter may not, in all likelihood will not, throw a bomb or hijack a plane, but neither will they consistently and unequivocally denounce those who do. Dr. Jasser and the reform-minded, the true moderates, will and do.

Judea Pearl, a professor at UCLA and the father of Daniel Pearl (the *Wall Street Journal* reporter who was slain, on camera, by Muslim terrorists for being an American and a Jew), put his finger on this whole difficult question quite perfectly. In the midst of the debate about the Ground Zero mosque, he wrote:

> The American Muslim leadership has had nine years to build up trust by taking proactive steps against the spread of anti-American terror-breeding ideologies, here and abroad.
>
> Evidently, however, a sizable segment of the American public is not convinced that this leadership is doing an effective job of confidence building.
>
> In public, Muslim spokespersons praise America as the best country for Muslims to live and practice their faith. But in

sermons, speeches, rallies, classrooms, conferences and books sold at those conferences, the narrative is often different. There, Noam Chomsky's conspiracy theory is the dominant paradigm, and America's foreign policy is one long chain of "crimes" against humanity, especially against Muslims.[27]

There are countless, almost daily, examples to support Pearl's point. Here's just one: In August 2010, the Muslim Public Affairs Council distributed a video to "work with a diversity of respected leaders and communities to tackle the issue of violent extremism head-on."[28] Among the speakers in the video is one Imam Zaid Shakir. While in *this* particular video he said nothing objectionable, here is precisely what the same Imam Shakir wrote less than a year before, just after the Fort Hood massacre:

> I begin by expressing my deepest condolences to the families of all of the dead and wounded. There is no legitimate reason for their deaths, just as I firmly believe there is no legitimate reason for the deaths of the hundreds of thousands of Iraqi and Afghani civilians who have perished as a result of those two conflicts. Even though I disagree with the continued prosecution of those wars, and even though I believe that the US war machine is the single greatest threat to world peace, I must commend the top military brass at Fort Hood, and President Obama for encouraging restraint and for refusing to attribute the crime allegedly perpetrated by Major Nidal Malik Hasan to Islam.[29]

Let's run this tape once more: (a) the deaths of American soldiers at Fort Hood, at the hand of Nidal Hasan, are akin to the deaths of civilians in Iraq and Afghanistan; (b) the U.S. military is not a liberator, but "the single greatest threat to world peace"; (c) Nidal Hasan "allegedly" committed a "crime"; and (d) refusing to link the terrorist act to Islam, even though the terrorist shouted "Allahu Akbar" as he killed his victims, is commendable. And a man who says this wants Americans to believe that he is tackling Muslim extremism "head-on"? This is the same "moderate" leader, it should be noted, who has also publicly stated, "Every Muslim who is honest would say, I would like to see America become a Muslim country."[30]

Professor Pearl concluded his analysis:

Overall, the message that emerges from this discourse is implicit, but can hardly be missed: When Muslim grievance is at question, America is the culprit and violence is justified, if not obligatory.

True, we have not helped Muslims in the confidence-building process. Treating homegrown terror acts as isolated incidents of psychological disturbances while denying their ideological roots has given American Muslim leaders the illusion that they can achieve public acceptance without engaging in serious introspection and responsibility sharing for allowing victimhood, anger and entitlement to spawn such acts.

We do no favor accepting as moderate or peaceful those who say one thing to one audience, seeking favor, and another to another audience, justifying anti-Americanism. Why, in response to Nidal Hasan's actions, is it so very difficult for a Muslim leader in America to say something simple, something like, "What Nidal Hasan did was horrific, and I condemn it without reservation or qualification," just as Christian leaders are quick to do when someone commits violence at an abortion clinic in the name of their faith? When we reach the point where someone who wants to be considered moderate can say that, and not pepper a statement of regret with qualification after qualification and condemnation of America after condemnation of America—in the very same paragraph—then we can more easily accept such spokesmen as leaders of moderate Islam.

A FALSE RESOLUTION TO THE TENSION

Unfortunately, the so-called mainstream civil and political American Muslim leadership groups from whom we so often hear do not trade in moral clarity. They seem more disposed toward convincing us of their moderation by redefining the word.

"Do remember you are there to fuddle him," the old, experienced devil, Screwtape, instructs his student in C. S. Lewis's *Screwtape Letters*. And fuddled we have become.

In another attempt to fight back against the supposed rise of Islamophobia in America, several of these so-called mainstream Muslim organizations convened in the waning days of August 2010 at various sites in Washington (from churches to the National Press Club) to unveil a new public relations campaign to prove just how mainstream Islam is. "The story of what mainstream American Muslims stand for has not been told effectively. We as Muslim Americans need to do a lot of changing and soul-searching," said the president of the Muslim American Public Affairs Council, Salam Al-Marayati.[31]

What changing and soul-searching were to be done remained unclear. That change and soul-searching were needed, especially by Al-Marayati, was, however, quite obvious. It was he who, just after the September 11 attacks, said the following in a radio interview: "If we're going to look at suspects, we should look to the groups that benefit the most from these kinds of incidents, and I think we should put the state of Israel on the suspect list because I think this diverts attention from what's happening in the Palestinian territories so that they can go on with their aggression and occupation and apartheid policies."[32] Israel as an apartheid state. No responsibility in Islam itself. No responsibility from a radicalized group of Muslims. And, oh yes, put Israel on the suspect list as culpable for 9/11.

This kind of verbal record has been repeated by Al-Marayati, as it has been by other so-called mainstream leaders, for "nine years," as Judea Pearl said. By August 2010 one had a hard time not being skeptical when the executive director of the Council on American Islamic Relations (CAIR) held a press conference the same week as Al-Marayati's statement, saying CAIR would be issuing a new public service announcement "with a message of religious inclusion and mutual understanding."[33] This was the same executive director who has more than once stated his support for Hamas and that the Muslim claim to Palestine is all of Israel.[34]

A certain level of distinction is noteworthy here. Devout Muslims in Saudi Arabia, as one example, are behaviorally different from devout Muslims in America; so, too, is the notion of moderation different in Saudi Arabia than it is here. It is not uncommon to see an unveiled Muslim woman in America. Quite the reverse, in fact. But in certain areas of the Middle East, as Reuel Marc Gerecht noted, such a sight "is a profound provocation."[35]

It would be preposterous for one to read us as believing in the existence of only one or two truly moderate Muslims, like Zuhdi Jasser, Muslims who are not followers or supporters of the Muslim Public Affairs Council or the Council on American Islamic Relations version of "moderate." There are plenty of Muslims who describe themselves as such and who are as disinterested in politics as they are in scrupulously attending to the details and precepts of Islam.

And, of course, in history there have been versions of that "elusive" moderate Islam that looks little like the Islam we see too much of today. Joshua Gilder pointed this out in a recent book review:

> [B]ack in the 8th and 9th centuries, when the rationalist Mu'tazilites dominated Islamic thought under Caliph al-Ma'mun. The period is often referred to as the "golden age of Islam," when that civilization produced some of its highest achievements in philosophy and science. It didn't last. In 849, the second year of the reign of Caliph Ja'afar al-Mutawakkil, the Mu'tazilites were overthrown. Holding Mu'tazilite beliefs became a crime punishable by death, and the decidedly anti-rationalist Ash'arites soon came to dominate the faith, as they would continue to do, in one form or another, through the modern era.[36]

There was a truly moderate, rationalist golden age—and it was defeated, by its own religion. That is the great concern here. There seems to be a terrible tension inherent to Islam. Where true moderation has existed, has it been the growth industry or has it been defeated and overthrown by the immoderate and the violent? We must resist the false resolution to the inherent tension by merely redefining moderation.

Perhaps discarding the whole analysis of "moderate Islam," as some have suggested, is the way out. We should, instead, be thinking about reform. Author Jon Meacham has written, "Islam needs reform. There are virulent elements of anti-Semitism and sexism abroad in the faith. There are, as we have noted, big strains of extreme anti-Western, specifically anti-American, hatred."[37] And from within Islam, Irshad Manji put it this way: "[M]oderate Muslims denounce terror that's committed in the name of Islam but they deny that religion has anything to do with it. . . . [R]eform-minded Muslims denounce terror that's committed in the name of Islam and acknowledge that our religion is used to inspire it."[38]

That is a distinction that allows a clear view of reality and also provides something of a solution. It tells us who and what we are dealing with as it simultaneously seeks a courageous honesty from the practicing Muslim advocate of his religion.

A PATH TO PEACE

A truly reformed Islam would lament but allow apostasy. It would support pluralism, denounce the application of Sharia law, prohibit polygamy and underage marriage, extend social and legal equality to nonbelievers, and inveigh against terrorism everywhere and always.[39]

Unless and until these kinds of conditions and statements can be met and agreed to, the case for doctrinal Islam, unreformed Islam, being a religion of peace has the status of "alleged" with several counts stacked up against it.

At first blush this may seem extreme, but let us qualify: at a certain level every religion requires the believers' adherence to its rules, its word of God. Christianity, in the words of Rev. Martin

Luther King Jr., for example, asks its adherents to be "extremists for peace." Orthodox Judaism is no different in asking and teaching adherence to a strict way of life that begins from one's very waking moment until the day is fully ended—and with extra rules and regulations on holidays.

That said, few of any sect perfectly adhere. There are a great number of Jews who are not Orthodox, just as there are a great number of Christians who do not follow all of their faith's—or even their pastors' or priests'—requests or rulings. Just as there are Jews who do not keep kosher or Christians who miss church on Sabbath, so, too, there are Muslims who do not practice all that their faith requires or practice it all the ways in which some say it is required. That could be mere imperfection, or it could be the start of reform.

Note the Fundamentalist Mormon Church and the Church of Latter Day Saints. Both call themselves Mormon. One believes in polygamy based on its original teachings; the other, the larger, has reformed and moved away from that, so as to comport with the norms of society and the laws of this country, and adapted it as part of its faith. One is fundamentalist; one is reformed. A lesson inheres.

It is for this reason that elsewhere in the book we refer to *radical Islam*. It is a descriptor, not an epithet. *Radical* means little more than *root*. Synonyms may very well include *fundamental* or *doctrinal*. But for us, *radical* says it just fine. The path to peace requires that radical Islam (or fundamental Islam or doctrinal Islam) reform itself.

What may be a "good Muslim" by modern Western standards may not be a "good Muslim" by Salafist or Sunni or Shiite standards. So then the question becomes, does an adherent of

Islam want to be a good Muslim by Western standards? Does one, in other words, want to live by our rules and not take up arms against his country because it does not follow Allah or rule by Sharia? Does one want to be a good Muslim by living his life by the nonviolent moral code found in much of the teachings of Islam? The answer is obvious: many do.

And they need to be cultivated.

8

THE WEST AND ISLAM

When we speak of the need for a reformed Islam, we do so knowing it is not an easy call or sell, and we leave the task to those Muslims whose religion it is, those like Dr. Zuhdi Jasser, who have the right within their religion to try.

As non-Muslims, we do, however, have a right to call—consistent with George Washington's requirement of "effectual support" for this country—for a more robust defense of the West and America. We also have the right to make such a call of Muslim and Arab defense groups in America, a call to put more Americans at ease by putting no asterisks in their statements about what they believe of Islam, terrorism, and America. Too many Muslim and Arab defense groups, just now, and for too long, have spoken out just as Professor Judea Pearl has described: with a double message or with qualified and qualifying defenses of their brethren.

Former British prime minister Tony Blair stood with America after 9/11 and learned much through the struggles that followed. He offered this helpful insight:

In the mind-set that is modern Islam, there is one spectrum, not several. At the furthest end of the spectrum are the extremists who advocate terrorism to further their goal of an Islamic state. . . . It is true they are few in number, but their sympathizers reach far further along the spectrum than we think. While many do not agree with terrorism, they "understand" why it is happening.

Still further along the spectrum are those who condemn the terrorists but in a curious and dangerous way buy into bits of their world view. They agree with the extremists that the U.S. is anti-Islam; they see the invasion of Afghanistan or Iraq as invasions of Muslim nations because they were Muslim nations. They see Israel as the symbol of Western anti-Islamic prejudice. This group stretches uncomfortably far into the middle of the spectrum.[1]

In a less squeamish time, such might have been called sympathizers. Blair does find another group, however, a stunted and mostly paralyzed majority:

[E]ven this group have not yet confidently found their way to articulating a thoroughly reformed and modernizing view of Islam. In other words, it is true they find the terrorism repugnant and they wish to be in alliance with the Western nations against it, but this does not yet translate into an alternative narrative for Islam that makes sense of its history and provides a coherent vision for its future.[2]

We can see all three parts of this spectrum here in America—the terrorists, those who claim the mantle of "moderate" (and are too easily anointed as such), and then the rest.

Denouncing events such as September 11, 2001, without qualification or categorization, denouncing terrorism, should be easy—likewise denouncing organizations like Hamas and Hezbollah for being terrorist. It should be an easy test for moderate Muslims to pass, one would think. But one would be surprised.

After delivering a lecture on Islam and the Middle East at the University of California at San Diego last year, conservative writer David Horowitz opened the floor for questions and answers. A female student in Islamic dress announced herself as a member of the Muslim Students Association, a supposed moderate group. She expressed disagreement with Horowitz, who then asked this American student if she agreed with or opposed Hamas. She would not answer. "Okay, I'll put it to you this way," said Horowitz. "I am a Jew. The head of Hezbollah has said that he hopes that we will [all] gather in Israel so he doesn't have to hunt us down [and kill us] globally. For or against it?" Calmly, in perfect English, this student at UCSD said, "For it."[3]

Most Muslims in America will not admit any such kind of support, and there are plenty of Muslims—outspoken and not—who have no truck with any of this and want to change Islam. Said Andrew C. McCarthy, they want to "evolve their faith into the light of ecumenical tolerance"; they are "Muslims who crave true religious liberty and reject [S]haria's repression."[4]

But, said McCarthy, "[t]hese reformist Muslims face a daunting challenge. . . . The power and money in the Islamic community is in the grip of the supremacists who pressure Muslims to resist assimilating in America."[5] And the power and the money in the world of Islamic teaching abroad, even here, is overwhelmingly in the hands of radical Muslims.

How to fight this?

ENTERING THE STRUGGLE

First, let us be clear about our enemy. Saying Islam is one thing (a religion of peace) when it is well another is a very good way to let down our guard. It is a very good way for people to be reticent to report things they may hear from Muslims (say, at a lecture on Islam at Bethesda Naval Hospital or in an airport security line in Alabama). And it is also a very good way for officials who get reports of suspicious Muslims to dismiss the worry, or believe they should be dismissed. It is a very good way, in other words, to numb ourselves.

If Islam is not a religion of peace, are our efforts in Iraq and Afghanistan (and possibly elsewhere) doomed? No. Just the opposite; a weakened resolve in those lands (and possibly elsewhere) will encourage the radical Islamists, while a perceptibly strong America will not.

Osama bin Laden may very well have believed America had invaded Muslim lands and relied on such a belief in declaring war on America, but at the same time he *thought* he could successfully declare war on America because of America's penchant for turning around and leaving places where it is attacked (as in Beirut and Somalia). He, and so many of his followers, believe in the strong horse/weak horse dichotomy. We should never cease in showing him and his followers what and who the strong horse really is.

It is worth noting here that tyrants do not generally attack where and when they think they will lose. At the same time they have made some of their greatest gains not only against weak countries but against countries that surrender. It should be no mystery as to why majority Muslim Arab countries ceased invading Israel by land after 1973. (They lost several previous conventional wars against Israel, including in 1973.) Nor, equally, should it be a mystery as to why terrorism grew against Israel subsequently: it was receiving more and more international sanction and defense.

In the midst of the struggle over New York's Ground Zero mosque, opponents were told that their actions would inflame Muslims abroad. But, which ultimately results in greater harm— acquiescence or resistance? Does standing up to immoderacy inflame enemies more than bowing and caving? The long and colorful history of peoples opposing tyranny shows that it is usually the gullible and weak who crumble, while the strong and resolute prevail.

In any event, the lawful governments of New York City and the United States permitted the building of that mosque while public opinion in America opposed it. What could douse the passions of inflamed Muslims abroad? If the answer is an America without dissent, well, that is no answer. If the answer is an America of tolerance, then that already exists with the many federally protected mosques in America. There is, for the record, no country with a Muslim majority or minority where Muslim rights are more respected than they are in America—not even, and especially, in the Middle East. If Muslims abroad do not understand that, the blame lies in the propaganda and the state-controlled media of their respective countries.

Blame also lies with so-called mainstream Muslim groups here who are too reticent to stand up for the American cause abroad, who continually denigrate this country and promote myths of intolerance. The Council on American Islamic Relations (CAIR), for example, has been continually opposed to the liberation of Iraq, and rather than praising the freedom it has given Arabs and Muslims, has called our efforts there "an occupation" and "not conducive to securing the basic rights of safety and liberty."[6] All of this feeds the misinformation and paranoia abroad that rattles around the mosques, television reports, and madrasahs.

The Council on American Islamic Relations, in the meantime, has been tied to Hamas in three separate federal court filings.[7] It is unconscionable that organizations like this can continue to get a free pass. The next time a spokesman from a group such as CAIR seeks special consideration on behalf of Islam or American Muslims, ask what he thinks of Hamas. Ask him if Hamas is a terrorist organization. Ask him if violence is ever justified against American or Israeli civilians. Ask him who was responsible for 9/11 and if any of it was justified in any way. We are in a war against radical Islam, and we have every right to know who is fighting that war and on what side.

Rather than create meaningless public service announcements and ads in this country, vaunting their peaceful intentions, mainstream Muslim and Arab groups here would do a better public service if they produced ads for their brethren abroad, promoting the virtues of American freedom and tolerance that they enjoy here, as well as ads explaining how our efforts abroad have given freedom to Muslims in other countries. Such efforts would be a good beginning—but it will take more.

Propaganda and conspiracy theories are nothing new in dictatorships and closed societies. Look back at Nazi Germany or Communist Russia. Look around at North Korea and Venezuela. The Middle East with its state-controlled media and paranoia-pushing clerics and schools is no different. One study commissioned by the UN found that "more books are translated into Spanish in a year than have been translated into Arabic in the past 1,000 years"[8] and that "the total number of books translated into

Arabic yearly . . . is about one-fifth of those translated in a small country like Greece.[9]

Does this make our liberation efforts abroad more difficult? Absolutely. Does it make them regretful? No. An Iraq without Saddam Hussein is an Iraq without a man who continually threatened the region, sponsored terrorists (and endowed suicide bombers), and led one of the worst torture regimes in the world. It is an Iraq that will not again, if we maintain our resolve there, see mass graves and mass starvation campaigns, efforts led by the government. There is great moment in the fact that two Iraqi prime ministers have addressed joint sessions of Congress since Hussein's ouster. As for the supposed terrorism and anger fueled by our efforts in Iraq, the two greatest Islamic terrorist attacks against the United States happened (1) before we liberated Iraq, and (2) again as we were on our way out, shortly after electing a U.S. president whose calling card was opposition to that war and who, once elected, ceased speaking of terrorism and apologized to the world for America's arrogance abroad. America as a strong force in the Middle East did not bring terror to our shores.

In all of this we need courage and clarity. An administration too skittish to mouth the word *terrorism* is little help in the fight. The same is true for civic organizations that cannot bring themselves to call a terrorist a terrorist—or, worse, have radicalized backgrounds and memberships of their own.

ENDING THE CULTURE OF GRIEVANCE

Our friend Debra Burlingame, whose brother, Chick, piloted Flight 77 until hijackers seized control and smashed it into the Pentagon, was asked several years ago if she missed the post-9/11 common sense. "Truthfully," she answered, "what I miss the most is the anger." We do too. Anger in war is healthy. Unlike rage, anger forces a certain clarity.

Not long after 9/11 we were, as a people, angry. Not vicious or violent, but angry. Today we have become sad and depressed and confused, and too many have replaced our concept of evil with all manner of diagnoses of syndromes and root causes. Too many of us have indeed either whitewashed the Islamic threat, turned our heads away from it, ignored it, or, in some cases, bought the excuse of it—namely that there are serious Muslim grievances with America and they are justified, or that, in the absence of such justification, they need appeasement and understanding.

It is not just the terrorist threat that we have to deal with now but also the grievance and apologetic culture under it, the culture that has taken such a strong hold in an increasingly enfeebled West. It may, in fact, prove the greater threat because it steals our greatest protection against terrorism: moral clarity. Where once our law and culture were based on assigning blame on a perpetrator of wrong, and personal responsibility was commonplace (as well as common sense), a new psychology has taken hold in Western culture. Where once we punished and fought, we now psychoanalyze and debate root causes. We, to borrow from Shakespeare, have made the wrong medicines of our great revenge to cure our deadly grief.

Let us begin a few years back. In 1992 a presidential candidate raised eyebrows when he uttered one of his most memorable lines: "I feel your pain." It spoke to a new sentiment in Western societies, that emotional empathy was the best a leader could offer an ailing body politic. Philip Rieff called it "the triumph of the therapeutic." Less than two decades later and we are suffering from empathy inflation. Whole populations are nursing supposed grievances and then expecting empathy and appeasement in exchange for not acting out—or using the same grievances as an excuse if they do.

Radical Islamists have taken the cue and played right to it. In 2005, in the wake of the worst attack in London since Hitler's Blitz, British prime minister Tony Blair met with two dozen local Muslim leaders to "address the root causes of the suicide bombings" that killed more than fifty innocent civilians and wounded more than seven hundred more. Who and what was responsible was obvious, the evil and barbaric actions of thugs and terrorists intoxicated by Islamic radicalism. But many of the so-called moderate Muslims who met with Blair played the grievance card that our culture dealt. Reported the *Washington Post*, "[T]he most prominent of Britain's Muslim moderates acknowledged strong disagreements among themselves, with the government and with radicals in their community over who or what is ultimately to blame for the attacks."[10]

Here in America, we, too, have mollycoddled supposedly "moderate" leaders, including members of the Saudi royal family and members of so-called Muslim civil rights organizations with troubling pasts and memberships. That *we* includes both Republican and Democratic presidents.

Churchill and Roosevelt took the war to the enemy. They did not ask their leaders about their grievances; their countries had heard them loudly and clearly enough through their actions. But throughout our culture, we have replaced what Lincoln called our "political religion," our dedication to knowing the causes of equality and liberty upon which we were founded, with a politics of religion, and race, and nationality, and culture. We have elevated individual grievances, ethnic thumb-sucking, and centuries-old resentments and envy above our mutual protection and our commonweal—a word whose rarity is only matched by the sentiment behind it. And we have elevated diversity above innocent life.

Some will dismiss such concerns as overwrought. But consider: Almost every time an analysis of terrorism is engaged in, from town-halls to symposia, an inevitable point will be made about "causes" and "justifications" and what the West or the United States can do or should do to help stop it. How *we* need to change, how *we* need to alter a certain policy, how *we* need to be more understanding, how *we* need to reexamine certain assumptions or practices. As if in some way—large or small—we are at fault or to blame.

We often hear that terrorism is caused because we are "occupying" Iraq. Just as often the rationale lies in our support of Israel. Of course, we were not "occupying" Iraq on September 11, 2001. Nor were we occupying Afghanistan, for that matter. And Great Britain has advocated more loudly than any other Western nation for Israeli withdrawal from the West Bank. It is not Iraq. It is not Israel. It is not Great Britain. And it is not America. It is a cor-rupt philosophy that, when acted upon, has led (and will lead) to untold slaughter and death.

CLARITY: MORAL AND FACTUAL

Let us be clear. We need not apologize for our survival, for fighting for our survival, or for the fact that the enemy struck us. Again, Tony Blair:

> What is the nature of the threat? It does not derive from some-
> thing we have done; there was no sense in which the West

sought a confrontation. This is essential to the argument. The attacks of Sept. 11 came to most of our citizens as a shock that was utterly unforeseen. Countries like America and Britain were not singling out Muslims for unfair treatment; and insofar as Muslims were caught up in generalized racism towards those of a different race or color, such attitudes were on the way out, not the way in.[11]

What is the problem, then? The problem is the current state of Islam. And it needs reform. As former federal judge and Attorney General Michael Mukasey put it, "There are many moderate Muslims, but there is simply no body of doctrine within Islam that provides a principled basis for condemning the 9/11 attacks."[12] There are too many violent teachings within Islam, taken up by too many practitioners and recruiters and apologists and defenders and redefiners of terrorism, to conclude otherwise. The problem is an enemy that cannot be negotiated with or appeased. The problem is an enemy so disconnected from the norms of usual warfare, so ready to attack almost any innocent, so willing to use any geography as a battlefield, it is impossible to assign any degree of moral fault to any party other than the enemy.

Ours is an enemy that straps bombs to children, that shoots nuns and burns churches in Africa, that blows up subways in Great Britain, that bombs trains in Spain and subways and airports in Russia, that kills filmmakers in Amsterdam, that puts prices on the heads of cartoonists from Copenhagen to Seattle, that goes on hotel and synagogue shooting rampages in India, that justifies honor killings from Amman, Jordan, to Irving, Texas, that threatens to wipe countries off of maps.

Our is an enemy whose institutes and universities teach that

"Jews are pigs and monkeys, that women and men must be stoned to death for adultery, or that Muslims must fight the world to spread their religion," as Tawfik Hamid, a former member of a terrorist organization, has put it.[13]

Ours is an enemy that knows no borders, and has supporters and sleeper cells the world over, including in America.

Ours is an enemy whose noxious doctrines are disseminated by those we call allies, such as the government of Saudi Arabia, which pays some "90 per cent of the expenses of the entire faith," according to author Lawrence Wright.[14] And those poisonous pieties are to be found in the materials distributed in some of America's largest mosques, saying such things as "'spill the blood' of apostates, polytheists, homosexuals, and adulterers." Such material "declares illegitimate any democratic state governed by 'infidel' laws; calls for Muslims to work to establish [S] haria states in the West through both aggressive *dawa* and militant jihad; promotes war to eradicate Israel; and are virulently anti-American."[15]

Ours is an enemy that uses civilian-filled airplanes as missiles.

And ours is an enemy that can be trained in the United States, give lectures on Islam, and then strap on his U.S. Army uniform and kill fellow Americans at a health center inside an army fort in Killeen, Texas.

In arguing that the problem is in the current state of Islam, where too many strong beliefs and spokesmen encourage and engender violence and terrorism, are we saying every Muslim is an enemy, every Muslim is the problem? Of course not. Millions of Muslims never take up arms, engage in terrorism, or defend such violence. They should, however, be the very first to loudly and unconditionally denounce their coreligionists who do. There are Muslims doing just this, and we have the highest praise for their courage and moral clarity. But there are not enough.

As Professor Bernard Lewis again reminded: "Most Muslims are not fundamentalists, and most fundamentalists are not terrorists, but most present-day terrorists are Muslims and proudly identify themselves as such." If there were an outbreak of terrorism where most terrorists were Christian or Jewish, those religions' members and leaders would hold rallies en masse denouncing their coreligionists in the strongest terms; those terrorists would be seen as isolated; they would be rebuked from within; and it would be known to all that they succored no favor with the leaders of those religions any more than with the vast majority of followers. That such a hypothetical is nearly unimaginable is itself defining and telling.

For saying this we make no apologies. Nor are we encouraging any private (or public) mistrust of our Muslim neighbors or friends or passersby. Not in any way. When and where American Muslims "demean themselves as good citizens," as George Washington put it and give their country "on all occasions their effectual support," then and there it is our duty and obligation to offer respect and friendship.

But for our foes—radical Islam and its supporters and its apologists—we must confront them head-on. This means, at a minimum, regaining the will not just to fight our enemy but also to call him by his proper name. To do otherwise is to repeat what we have already done, which is to "discourage the American people's natural reaction to their attackers," as Professor Angelo Codevilla put it.[16] We will not prevail by underestimating, appeasing, or ignoring our enemy.

As we give our enemy the honesty and renewed scrutiny he

warrants, we must also recommit to our shared American heritage and values. One cannot fight something with nothing, particularly something as strong as radical Islam. An invigorated sense of American identity and unity is needed.

We are today in the fight of our lives—not only against a theocratically fueled enemy that despises everything we stand for but also against a thickened veil at home, a veil that has covered the very light we need in order to see the enemy for what he is and to see ourselves for what and who we are.

We can be the author and finisher of our own destruction, or we can push back against the culture of death abroad and the culture of nihilism at home. The choice is ours. We have been here before. We have been in the fight of our lives at various times before in our history, commencing with our very own beginning. Winning those fights, as well as how we won those fights, has been a singular American privilege and lesson to ourselves in times past. It has also been the cause of freedom for others. To give it up now, to surrender now, is a betrayal of us and of others.

Lifting our veil and engaging the fight, as both a matter of military and civic strength, is our great task. It begins with knowing the enemy and knowing ourselves. The time to take this up is now. It cannot wait.

EPILOGUE:
BEGINNING THE
GREAT RELEARNING

THE GELDED AGE

If we are to prevail, we have some import work of reconstitution to do. The problem we face is severe and it is tough because it thrives in a chasm, a cultural vacuum. The so-called grievances and doctrines of radical Islam are contrasted to nothing. There is no other side of the scale; there is almost no teaching of what we do right; there is almost no recognition of the wisdom and virtue of our own cause from our founding up until today. This collective ignorance and amnesia is nothing short of a crisis.

The defense of the West and America has long been too weak—in our schools as much as in our entertainment and from our own leaders. With a feeble sense of the Western self, is it any wonder that lost and thirsty youth looking for something firm in which to believe can be attracted to the strong message of Islam?

We have seen this phenomenon growing in Europe and worry about it here in America.

Having denied our children an understanding, knowledge, and appreciation for our Western and American ethics and history (which includes the teachings of equality and liberty, equanimity, and charity), we have ended up where we are today. This failure, more than anything else, could prove the West's undoing. In America, one can graduate from any of America's top colleges and not take a single course in American history. Meanwhile, our political scientists and historians teach that our founding was racist or classist or elitist, at best. "[Y]ou can't assimilate with a nullity—which is what multiculturalism is," said Mark Steyn. "So, if Islamist extremism is the genie you're trying to put back in the bottle, it doesn't help to have smashed the bottle."[1]

Indeed, we have smashed the bottle of national identity and proper and purposeful assimilation—in both the United States and Britain, as well other European nations. A great relearning is required if we are to endure and be safe.

Historian David McCullough testified before Congress in 2005 that U.S. history is the "worst subject" in our nation's classrooms. In the same hearing, U.S. Senator (and former secretary of education) Lamar Alexander cited the results of the National Assessment of Educational Progress. "[F]ewer students have just a basic understanding of American history than have a basic understanding of any other subject which we test," he said, "including math, science and reading."[2] Our children's grades are naturally as low as our national sense of self—the two are linked.

Meanwhile, the uber ethic of diversity replaces history with "social studies," a feckless and disappointing substitute that, as

Stanford professor William Damon noted, emphasizes "tolerance for non-Western cultures and criticism of our own."[3] While we criticize ourselves, we do not teach, he said, "about parts of the world that have not been blessed by freedom and democracy." We do not teach "how women feel in cultures that keep them illiterate and disenfranchised, force them to wear smothering clothes or undergo involuntary genital surgery, punish them when they are raped, and threaten them with harm when their families cannot afford huge dowries." We do not contrast those societies "with societies where everyone gets to vote, protest, join unions, start businesses, marry and divorce at will, choose partners out of affection, not coercion, worship or not worship as they wish."

In short, we no longer teach, said Damon, "a sense of how freedom has been won in some places and lost in others. How American rights were forged through suffering in Valley Forge and Selma; how utopian Russian dreams slipped away into tyranny; how German democracy was brought down by terrorism and divisiveness in the Weimar years; how Japan succumbed to its leaders' militarism and expansionism." And we do not teach the American role in reforming itself while fighting the various evils arrayed against us.

We have made aliens in our country by alienating ourselves and our children from our history and our cause. Not only do many of our children no longer study our history at all; too many who do, study it as an oppressive story of misery, exploitation, and injustice. Looking for sustenance, they are served thin gruel in our nation's classrooms. Is it any wonder, then, that some poor souls, when offered a strong helping of identity in something else, of righteousness in some cause, are drawn to it? Say what you will of them, but nationalist supremacy, racial superiority, and Islamic fundamentalism are all strong brews, particularly for the immature and uncritical, and they can fill hungry and lost souls.

That's the cost of denigrating our own story. Said C. S. Lewis, "We laugh at honor and are shocked to find traitors in our midst. We castrate and bid the geldings be fruitful."[4]

An uncertain West with an embarrassing history stands little chance against the power and appeal of a strong, if noxious, ideology. Combine all of this with the "rage" that naturally follows from the catalogue of the evil actions of the West, and we begin to "understand root causes" for some. And radical Islam is there in the waiting, in the preaching, and for the taking.

OUR POLITICAL RELIGION

It is now time to roll off our national and international couches, stand erect, and direct all citizens, Muslim and non-Muslim alike, to the source of a better medicine, one once seen as strong, curative, and worth fighting for. It is known as our founding creed. There are, indeed, self-evident truths and rights, among which are the equality and freedom of all humans—women, Jews, and infidels among them—and they are entitled to, nay, already endowed with those rights. And yet, we no longer speak or teach the language of such moral absolutism (such exquisite extremism) with the moral conviction that inspires.

Radical Muslim leaders slake that thirst with their *immoral* absolutism. That is why there is a strong Islamist appeal to the John Walker Lindhs, Adam Ghadans, Nidal Hasans, David

Headleys, Anwar al-Awlakis, and God knows how many other lost souls among us. They follow a strong and stern teaching to a perverted end. And they have teachers who believe in that end and lead them to it. Those teachers offer a cause for which to live *and die.*

It is in our power to breed heroes and statesmen, just as much as terrorists and traitors. We breed by both example and instruction. If we are to cultivate heroes and statesmen, then we must recommit ourselves to the founding creed, to the philosophies of statecraft and soulcraft that have undergirded our nation for generations.

The word *religion* comes from the same root that supplies the word *ligatures* and *ligaments*; it means that which ties and binds. This is why Abraham Lincoln would speak of our "political religion" as that which motivated the founding generation and as that to which we needed to return in his day—and beyond. His worry then, as ours today, was the vanishing and vanished frame of reference about that political religion. Revisit Lincoln's Lyceum speech and it is uncanny to read what Lincoln saw then in light of what so many of us see today. He pointed to the problem of the fading story of our own history, the amnesia about the lessons that had inspired us to found a nation dedicated to strong and important things. To be sure, Lincoln lamented our unlearning and our amnesia. He was worried. But he was no pessimist. He concluded his Lyceum speech by saying that the scenes and teachings from our Revolution and founding

> were the pillars of the temple of liberty; and now, that they
> have crumbled away, that temple must fall, *unless* we, their
> descendants, supply their places with other pillars, hewn

from the solid quarry of sober reason. Passion has helped us; but can do so no more. It will in future be our enemy. Reason, cold, calculating, unimpassioned reason, must furnish all the materials for our future support and defence. Let those materials be moulded into general intelligence, sound morality, and in particular, a reverence for the constitution and laws. . . .

Upon these let the proud fabric of freedom rest, as the rock of its basis; and as truly as has been said of the only greater institution, "the gates of hell shall not prevail against it."[5]

Today, just when we need it most, just as we are threatened by and are at war with a strong theology dedicated to violence on a massive scale against us, we seem to have abandoned our political religion, our cause, our learning, the public faith in and of our own country.

Is it too late to recapture the forces of composition over the forces of decomposition? We will know soon enough, when the next act of terrorism takes place. Will it be at the hands of an American we may be instructing here, or a Brit in London? After all, these murderers take their instruction seriously.

We may soon find out whether we will take seriously our great moral and intellectual inheritance and so determine whether we indeed have the will, and ability, to not only call this a war but to identify our enemy and to win it as well. Or, in the long run, will we prove to be the authors of our own undoing?[6]

Let us avoid that suicide, let us call good and evil by their proper names. Let us know the enemy as the enemy and not hide behind sophisticated philosophies and synonyms and pseudonyms. And let us know ourselves for who we are and what we've done, for citizens here as well as for the immiserated abroad. Let the doublespeak and nonspeak end and the great relearning and rededication begin.

To win the fight of our lives, we must do nothing less.

ACKNOWLEDGMENTS

This book and our judgment about the matters we write about would not have been possible without the support, from the very beginning—in 2001 up until now—of Lawrence Kadish of New York. He is a man singularly focused on the most important things in both public and private life, first and foremost our great country and its children. There is not enough space here or elsewhere to thank him for his contributions to our country or to our work.

Brian Kennedy, president of the Claremont Institute, is one of the most important public intellectuals in America. He has implicitly and explicitly been urging us to put our thoughts on paper for a very long time. He, along with the Claremont Institute, has been a constant encouragement and source of support—intellectual and otherwise.

There is no way to properly thank Noreen Burns, with whom we have worked for more than thirty-four years collectively. Without her, very little gets done. Her dedication to our mutual work is boundless.

Dr. Zuhdi Jasser is a man who, if we win this war, will deserve much of the intellectual credit. A tireless worker for his country, in uniform and out, he has understood the threat and has braved the slings and arrows of his coreligionists and others to speak truth to power. He has educated us immeasurably, as he educates anyone who gives him the time to hear what he has to say and read what he has to write. To us he is a true hero.

Neal Kozodoy and David Gelernter shared their time and great brains in thinking through some of the tougher issues here. They are true American treasures and intellects we simply cannot imagine this country surviving without.

No serious study of the terrorist threat to America and the West can take place without studying the work of Steve Emerson. He has been at it for longer than most, and to ignore his work is to imperil ourselves. He is a brave and serious scholar and investigator who helps show the way and is deserving of nothing less than the Presidential Medal of Freedom.

And what can we say of Andy McCarthy? He has imprisoned terrorists and he has alerted all of those willing to pay attention to the greatest threats—internal and external—that lie in wait, from the intellectual to the actual. He is, first and foremost, a teacher and the teacher America very much needs just now.

Kathryn Jean Lopez has been a constant and continued presence in our lives for more years than we can count—urging, cajoling, forcing us to think through issues we otherwise might have neglected. For all her work with us and others, we thank her.

Joel Miller, our editor, is the best editor any writer or any two writers could have; he is also a total pleasure to work with. He jumped up in favor of this manuscript the moment we began suggesting it, and he has improved it every step of the way.

Finally, but by no means lastly, to our wives, the two "E's" as we call them—Elayne Bennett and Elaine Leibsohn. Their support can never be repaid or properly acknowledged, though we try.

NOTES

Epigraphs

1. Martina Stewart, "Casey: I'm 'Concerned' About Backlash Against Muslim Soldiers," http://politicalticker.blogs.cnn .com/2009/11/08/casey-im-concerned-about-possible-backlash-against-muslim-soldiers/?fbid=lajeVk_ZHid (accessed July 4, 2010).
2. Quoted in Melvin Richter, *The Political Theory of Montesquieu* (New York: Cambridge University Press, 1977), 52.

Introduction

1. "The Faisal Shazad transcript," *New York Post*, http://www .nypost.com/p/news/local/manhattan/read_the_faisal_shahzad_transcript_zDoUXlGEMoqZMwzsIRrlkM (accessed November 18, 2010).

Chapter 1

1. "Teaching with Documents: 'A Date Which Will Live in Infamy,'" http://www.archives.gov/education/lessons/day-of-infamy/ (accessed July 4, 2010).
2. Walter Shapiro, "Anti-anti-war Crowd Dreams Up a Disloyal Opposition," *USA Today*, March 13, 2002, http://www.usatoday .com/news/opinion/shapiro/610.htm (accessed July 4, 2010).
3. "Afghanistan," http://www.pollingreport.com/afghan.htm (accessed October 29, 2010).

4. "Maj. Nidal M. Hasan," *Washington Post*, November 7, 2009, http://www.washingtonpost.com/wp-dyn/content/article/2009/11/06/AR2009110601978.html (accessed July 5, 2010); and James Dao, "Suspect Was 'Mortified' About Deployment," *New York Times*, November 6, 2009, http://www.nytimes.com/2009/11/06/us/06suspect.html (accessed July 5, 2010).

5. Ibid.

6. James C. McKinley Jr. and James Dao, "Fort Hood Gunman Gave Signals Before His Rampage," *New York Times*, November 9, 2009, http://www.nytimes.com/2009/11/09/us/09reconstruct.html?_r=1&pagewanted=2 (accessed July 5, 2010).

7. "Hasan on Islam," *Washington Post*, http://www.washingtonpost.com/wp-dyn/content/gallery/2009/11/10/GA2009111000920.html (accessed July 5, 2010).

8. Ibid.

9. Ibid.

10. Ibid.

11. Daniel Zwerdling, "Walter Reed Officials Asked: Was Hasan Psychotic?" NPR, November 11, 2009, http://www.npr.org/templates/story/story.php?storyId=120313570 (accessed July 5, 2010).

12. Ibid.

13. Ibid.

14. Joseph Rhee, Mary-Rise Abraham, Anna Schecter, and Brian Ross, "Officials: Major Hasan Sought 'War Crimes' Prosecution of U.S. Soldiers," ABC News, November 16, 2009, http://abcnews.go.com/print?id=9019904 (accessed July 10, 2010).

15. Mark Schone, Joseph Rhee, Mary-Rose Abraham, and Anna Schecter, "Major Hasan Dined with Jihad Hobbyist," ABC News, November 17, 2009, http://abcnews.go.com/print?id=9100187 (accessed July 10, 2010).

16. McKinley and Dao, "Fort Hood Gunman Gave Signals Before His Rampage," http://www.nytimes.com/2009/11/09/us/09reconstruct.html?_r=2&pagewanted=print (accessed July 10, 2010).

17. Richard Esposito, Mary-Rose Abraham, and Rhonda Schwartz, "Major Hasan: Soldier of Allah; Many Ties to Jihad Web Sites,"

ABC News, November 12, 2009, http://abcnews.go.com/Blotter/
hasan-multiple-mail-accounts-officials/story?id=9065692
(accessed July 10, 2010).

18. Richard Esposito, Rehab El-Buri, and Brian Ross, "From
Yemen, Anwar Awlaki Helped Inspire Fort Dix, Toronto Plots,"
ABC News, November 11, 2009, http://abcnews.go.com/
print?id=9055322 (accessed July 12, 2010).

19. The chronology of public events and statements in Hasan's life is
well documented in one place by Middle East and Islam scholar
Daniel Pipes here: http://www.danielpipes.org/7763/major-nidal-
hasan-islamist-life (accessed July 18, 2010).

20. "General Casey: Diversity Shouldn't Be Casualty of Fort
Hood," Reuters, November 8, 2009, http://blogs.reuters.com/
frontrow/2009/11/08/general-casey-diversity-shouldnt-be-
casualty-of-fort-hood/ (accessed July 18, 2010).

21. Michael Barone, "A Tale of Two Nations," *U.S. News*, May 4, 2003,
http://www.usnews.com/usnews/opinion/articles/030512/12pol
.htm (accessed July 18, 2010).

22. *Protecting the Force: Lessons from Fort Hood*, http://www.defense
.gov/pubs/pdfs/DOD-ProtectingTheForce-Web_Security_
HR_13jan10.pdf (accessed July 18, 2010).

23. Ibid.

24. Ralph Peters, "Hood Massacre Report Gutless and Shameful,"
New York Post, January 17, 2010, http://www.nypost.com/p/news/
opinion/opedcolumnists/hood_massacre_report_gutless_and_
yaUphSPCoMs8ux4lQdtyGM (accessed July 18, 2010).

25. "Protecting the Force: Lessons from Fort Hood."

26. Ibid.

27. Ibid.

28. Ibid.

29. Peters, "Hood Massacre Report Gutless and Shameful."

30. "Final Recommendations of the Ft. Hood Follow-on Review," the
Secretary of Defense, August 18, 2010, http://www.defense.gov/
news/d20100820FortHoodFollowon.pdf.

31. Nancy Youssef and Mark Seibel, "Fort Hood Shooting Revealed
Multiple Military Security Lapses," McClatchy.com, August
20, 2010, http://www.mcclatchydc.com/2010/08/20/99497/

fort-hood-shooting-revealed-multiple.html (accessed October 29, 2010).

Chapter 2

1. Rick Hampson, "9/11 recruits: They Enlisted When USA Was Under Fire," *USA Today*, September 8, 2005, http://www.usatoday .com/news/nation/2005-09-08-9-11-recruits-cover_x.htm (accessed July 18, 2010).
2. Ryan Lizza, "Making It: How Chicago Shaped Obama," *New Yorker*, July 21, 2008, http://www.newyorker.com/ reporting/2008/07/21/080721fa_fact_lizza?currentPage=all (accessed July 18, 2010).
3. "Bin Laden's Fatwa," PBS.org, http://www.pbs.org/newshour/ terrorism/international/fatwa_1996.html (accessed July 18, 2010).
4. "John Miller's 1998 Interview with Osama Bin Laden (Why We Fight Reminder), *Free Republic*, January 31, 2003, http://www .freerepublic.com/focus/news/833647/posts (accessed July 18, 2010).
5. "Transcript of Osama bin Laden Videotape, "December 13, 2001, http://www.greatdreams.com/osama_tape.htm (accessed July 18, 2010).
6. Norman Podhoretz, *World War IV: The Long Struggle Against Islamofascism* (New York: First Vintage, 2008), 29.
7. Ibid.
8. Alan Dershowitz, *Why Terrorism Works* (New Haven: Yale University Press), 57. See also: http://www.jewishvirtuallibrary .org/jsource/Terrorism/usvictims.html (accessed July 18, 2010).
9. Robert Pear, "U.S. Agrees to Talks with P.L.O, Saying Arafat Accepts Israel and Renounces All Terrorism," *New York Times*, December 15, 1988, http://www.nytimes.com/1988/12/15/world/ us-agrees-talks-with-plo-saying-arafat-accepts-israel-renounces-all-terrorism.html (accessed July 20, 2010).
10. Jeff Jacoby, "Hezbollah Is Our Enemy, Too," July 30, 2006, http:// www.jeffjacoby.com/259/hezbollah-is-our-enemy-too (accessed July 20, 2010).

11. Ibid.
12. Bernard Lewis, *Faith and Power* (New York: Oxford University Press, 2010), 166.
13. Ibid.
14. "Secretary of Defense Maintenance Awards," U.S. Department of Defense, http://www.defense.gov/speeches/speech.aspx?speechid=462 (accessed July 20, 2010).
15. "Transcript of President Bush's Address," CNN.com, September 21, 2001, http://archives.cnn.com/2001/US/09/20/gen.bush.transcript/ (accessed July 20, 2010).
16. Ibid.
17. Ibid.
18. "George W. Bush: Address at Islamic Center of Washington," American Rhetoric, http://www.americanrhetoric.com/speeches/gwbush911islamispeace.htm (accessed October 29, 2010).
19. Annafrid Vincze, "Afgan Restaurant Counts on Tradition," March 30, 2006, http://www.afghankabobrestaurant.com/reviews.php (accessed July 20, 2010).
20. http://www.fbi.gov/about-us/cjis/ucr/hate-crime/2001.
21. http://www.fbi.gov/about-us/cjis/ucr/hate-crime/2002.
22. "Miss Michigan USA 2011," http://www.missmichiganusa.com/michiganusa.html (accessed August 18, 2010).
23. *Saudi Publications on Hate Ideology Invade American Mosques*, Center for Religious Freedom: Freedom House, http://www.freedomhouse.org/uploads/special_report/45.pdf (accessed July 20, 2010).
24. Daniel Pipes, "Bush Declared War on Radical Islam," October 11, 2005, http://www.danielpipes.org/3026/bush-declares-war-on-radical-islam (accessed July 20, 2010).
25. "White House Apologizes for Using 'Crusade' to Describe War on Terrorism," *Daily Transcript*, September 18, 2001, http://www.sddt.com/News/article.cfm?SourceCode=20010918ll (accessed July 20, 2010).
26. "Franklin D. Roosevelt D-Day Prayer," http://www.historyplace.com/speeches/fdr-prayer.htm (accessed July 20, 2010).

Chapter 3

1. "Iraq and the War on Terrorism," Al Gore, September 23, 2002, http://www.commonwealthclub.org/archive/02/02-09gore-speech.html (accessed July 20, 2010).
2. Ibid.
3. William J. Bennett, *A Century Turns* (Nashville: Thomas Nelson Publishing, 2010), 179.
4. Ibid., 179–80.
5. Christopher Hitchens, *Hitch-22* (New York: Hatchette Book Group), 297–98.
6. Bennett, *A Century Turns*, 176.
7. Ibid.
8. Ibid., 203.
9. William J. Bennett, *Why We Fight* (Washington, DC: Regnery Publishing, 2003), 4.
10. Paul Berman, *The Flight of the Intellectuals* (Brooklyn: Melville House Publishing, 2010), 21.
11. Ibid., 24.
12. "Tariq Ramadan," http://www.discoverthenetworks.org/individualProfile.asp?indid=1884 (accessed July 20, 2010).
13. Steven Emerson, "Tariq Ramadan: The Case of the Grand Deception," April 1, 2005, http://www.investigativeproject .org/339/tariq-ramadan-the-case-of-the-grand-deception (accessed July 20, 2010).
14. Ibid.
15. Berman, *The Fight of the Intellectuals*, 197.
16. Ibid., 193.
17. Ibid., 36.
18. Ibid., 31.
19. Ibid., 33.
20. Ibid., 189.
21. "Sheik Yusuf al-Qaradawi: Theologian of Terror," ADL.org, August 4, 2009, http://www.adl.org/NR/exeres/788C5421-70E3-4E4D-BFF4-9BE14E4A2E58,DB7611A2-02CD-43AF-8147-649E26813571,frameless.htm (accessed July 20, 2010).

22. Berman, *The Fight of the Intellectuals*, 214.
23. Ibid.
24. Ibid., 215.
25. Ibid.
26. Thomas L. Friedman, "Can We Talk?" *New York Times*, July 17, 2010, http://www.nytimes.com/2010/07/18/opinion/18friedman.html?_r=1&ref=thomaslfriedman (accessed July 21, 2010).
27. Jeff Jacoby, "Hezbollah Is Our Enemy, Too," July 30, 2006, http://www.jeffjacoby.com/259/hezbollah-is-our-enemy-too (accessed July 21, 2010).
28. Ibid.
29. Ibid.
30. "The Al-Qaeda-Hezbollah Relationship," Fighting Terrorism, October 26, 2009, http://www.fightingterrorism.info/the-al-qaeda-hezbollah-relationship.html (accessed July 21, 2010).
31. Borzou Daragahi, "Lebanese Ayatollah Offers Advice for 'Modern Shiites,'" *Los Angeles Times*, February 6, 2008, http://articles.latimes.com/2008/feb/06/world/fg-fadlallah6 (accessed July 21, 2010).
32. Uzi Mahnaimi, Hala Jaber, and Jon Swain, "Israel Kills Terror Chief with Headrest Bomb," *Sunday Times* (UK), February 17, 2008, http://www.timesonline.co.uk/tol/news/world/middle_east/article3382343.ece (accessed July 21, 2010).
33. Ibid.
34. Friedman, "Can We Talk?"
35. Ibid.
36. "We Could Provide a Million Suicide Bombers in 24 Hours," *Telegraph* (UK), September 4, 2002, http://www.telegraph.co.uk/news/worldnews/middleeast/lebanon/1400406/We-could-provide-a-million-suicide-bombers-in-24-hours.html (accessed July 21, 2010).
37. Friedman, "Can We Talk?"
38. "Lawmaker raises questions about Ground Zero mosque," http://www.usatoday.com/news/nation/2010-07-13-trade-center-mosque_N.htm (accessed November 19, 2010).
39. Ibid.

40. "Prominent American Muslims Denounce Terror Committed in the Name of Islam," http://www.islamfortoday.com/60minutes.htm (accessed August 18, 2010).
41. "Feisal Abdul Rauf Tape: U.S. Has More Blood on Its Hands Than Al-Qaida," AOL News, August 23, 2010, http://www.investigativeproject.org/2122/feisal-abdul-rauf-tape-us-has-more-blood-on-its (accessed October 29, 2010).
42. Tom Topousis, "Imam Terror Error," *New York Post*, June 19, 2010, http://www.nypost.com/p/news/local/manhattan/imam_terror_error_efmizkHuBUaVnfuQcrcabL (accessed August 18, 2010).
43. Michael Kinsley, "Cordoba House, Charles Krauthammer, and the First Amendment," *Atlantic Wire*, August 16, 2010, http://www.theatlanticwire.com/editor-at-large/view/article/Cordoba-House-Charles-Krauthammer-and-the-First-Amendment-44 (accessed August 18, 2010).
44. Roland Martin, "I Love Jesus, the Constitution and Can Support the Building of a Muslim Mosque," August 20, 2010, http://www.rolandsmartin.com/blog/index.php/2010/08/20/i-love-jesus-the-constitution-and-can-support-the-building-of-a-muslim-mosque/ (accessed August 18, 2010).
45. Abraham H. Foxman, "The Mosque at Ground Zero," *Huffington Post*, August 2, 2010, http://www.huffingtonpost.com/abraham-h-foxman/the-mosque-at-ground-zero_b_668020.html (accessed August 18, 2010).
46. Javier C. Hernandez, "Planned Sign of Tolerance Bringing Division Instead," *New York Times*, July 13, 2010, http://www.nytimes.com/2010/07/14/nyregion/14center.html?_r=1 (accessed August 18, 2010).
47. "Remarks by the President at Iftar Dinner," The White House, August 13, 2010, http://www.whitehouse.gov/the-press-office/2010/08/13/remarks-president-iftar-dinner-0 (accessed August 18, 2010).
48. http://abcnews.go.com/Politics/wireStory?id=11398588.
49. Sheryl Gay Stolberg, "Obama Strongly Backs Islam Center Near 9/11 Site," *New York Times*, August 13, 2010, http://www.nytimes

.com/2010/08/14/us/politics/14obama.html (accessed August 18, 2010).

50. "Under Fire, Obama Clarifies Support for Ground Zero Mosque," Fox News, August 14, 2010, http://www.foxnews.com/politics/2010/08/14/obamas-support-ground-zero-mosque-draws/ (accessed August 18, 2010).

51. "CNN Opinion Research Poll," http://i2.cdn.turner.com/cnn/2010/images/08/11/rel11a.pdf (accessed August 18, 2010).

52. "Growing Number of Mosques in New York City," Fox News, August 8, 2010, http://www.foxnewsinsider.com/2010/08/09/growing-number-of-mosques-in-new-york-city/ (accessed August 18, 2010).

53. Bobby Ghosh, "Islamophobia: Does America Have a Muslim Problem?" *Time*, August 19, 2010, http://www.time.com/time/nation/article/0,8599,2011798,00.html (accessed October 3, 2010).

54. Raheel Raza and Tarek Fatah, "Mischief in Manhattan," *Ottawa Citizen*, August 17, 2010, http://www.ottawacitizen.com/news/Mischief+Manhattan/3370303/story.html#ixzz0wcZNOGAS (accessed August 18, 2010).

55. Jennifer Fermino, "Muslim Miss USA: Move the Mosque!" *New York Post*, August 21, 2010, http://www.nypost.com/p/news/local/manhattan/muslim_miss_usa_move_the_mosque_C0VlK0arNhi oO9OPJ560FO#ixzz0xGIZr4Sr (accessed August 18, 2010).

Chapter 4

1. "Under Secretary for Public Diplomacy and Public Affairs," U.S. Department of State, http://www.state.gov/r/ (accessed July 20, 2010).

2. William J. Bennett, "The Forces of Decomposition and the War on Terror," The Claremont Institute, September 7, 2005, http://www.claremont.org/publications/pubid.442/pub_detail.asp (accessed July 20, 2010).

3. William J. Bennett, "We Must Fight Now," *National Review*, March 11, 2003, http://article.nationalreview.com/268150/we-must-fight-now/william-j-bennett (accessed July 20, 2010).

4. Eric Schmitt and Thom Shanker, "Washington Recasts Terror

War as 'Struggle,'" http://www.nytimes.com/2005/07/26/world/
americas/26iht-terror.html (accessed July 21, 2010).

5. Ibid.

6. Elisabeth Bumiller, "With a Few Humble Words, Bush Silences
His Texas Swagger," *New York Times*, May 27, 2006, http://www
.nytimes.com/2006/05/27/washington/27lingo.html (accessed
August 18, 2010).

7. Karl Rove, "My Biggest Mistake in the White House," *Wall Street
Journal*, July 15, 2010, http://online.wsj.com/article/SB1000142
4052748704518904575365793062101552.html?mod=WSJ_hps_
SECONDTopStories (accessed July 26, 2010).

8. Ibid.

9. Andrew C. McCarthy, "Karl Rove's Mea Culpa," *National Review*,
July 15, 2010, http://article.nationalreview.com/print/?q=Nzkz
OGU1ZjA3YTYyZTAxNTUwMTI0ZWM4OWE3ZTM1OWM=
(accessed July 26, 2010).

10. Ibid.

11. "Report on the U.S. Intelligence Community's Prewar Intelligence
Assessments on Iraq," http://www.globalsecurity.org/intell/
library/congress/2004_rpt/iraq-wmd-intell_toc.htm (accessed
July 27, 2010).

12. "Bush's Final Approval Rating: 22 Percent," CBS News, January
16, 2009, http://www.cbsnews.com/stories/2009/01/16/opinion/
polls/main4728399.shtml (accessed July 26, 2010).

13. Cori E. Dauber and Peter D. Feaver, "Body Bags Alone Won't
Dampen American Morale," *USA Today*, March 20, 2002, 15A.

14. "Full Transcript: Saddleback Presidential Forum, Sen. Barack
Obama, John McCain; Moderated by Rick Warren," August
17, 2008, http://www.clipsandcomment.com/2008/08/17/
full-transcript-saddleback-presidential-forum-sen-barack-obama-
john-mccain-moderated-by-rick-warren/ (accessed July 21, 2010).

15. Ibid.

Chapter 5

1. "'Glenn Beck': Obama Administration Damaging U.S. Relations
with Israel?" Fox News, June 4, 2010, http://www.foxnews.com/

story/0,2933,594022,00.html (accessed October 3, 2010).

2. Hossam el-Hamalawy, "Right Time, Wrong Place," *New York Times*, June 3, 2009, http://www.nytimes.com/2009/06/03/opinion/03alHamalawy.html (accessed July 28, 2010).

3. M. Zuhdi Jasser, "Obama's Speech in Egypt Must Highlight the Plight of Reformers and the Threat of Islamism," *Huffington Post*, June 4, 2009, http://www.huffingtonpost.com/m-zuhdi-jasser/obamas-speech-in-egypt-mu_b_210975.html (accessed October 29, 2010).

4. "'Glenn Beck': Obama Administration Damaging U.S. Relations with Israel?"

5. "Napolitano Avoids Terror Terminology," CBS News, February 24, 2009, http://www.cbsnews.com/stories/2009/02/24/national/main4826437.shtml (accessed July 29, 2010).

6. "One Team, One Mission, Securing Our Homeland," Homeland Security, http://www.dhs.gov/xlibrary/assets/DHS_StratPlan_FINAL_spread.pdf (accessed July 29, 2010).

7. "Away from the Politics of Fear," *Spiegel Online*, March 16, 2009, http://www.spiegel.de/international/world/0,1518,613330,00.html (accessed July 29, 2010).

8. Michelle Malkin, "You Might Be a Radicalized Rightwing Extremist If . . ." April 15, 2009, http://michellemalkin.com/2009/04/15/you-might-be-a-radicalized-rightwing-extremist-if/ (accessed July 29, 2010).

9. Eli Lake, "Napolitano Stands by Controversial Report," *Washington Times*, April 16, 2009, http://www.washingtontimes.com/news/2009/apr/16/napolitano-stands-rightwing-extremism/ (accessed July 29, 2010).

10. "Rightwing Extremism: Current Economic and Political Climate Fueling Resurgence in Radicalization and Recruitment," http://www.wnd.com/images/dhs-rightwing-extremism.pdf (accessed July 29, 2010).

11. Ibid.

12. Scott Wilson and Al Kamen, "'Global War on Terror' Is Given New Name," *Washington Post*, March 25, 2009, http://www.washingtonpost.com/wp-dyn/content/article/2009/03/24/AR2009032402818.html (accessed July 29, 2010).

13. Ibid.
14. Ibid.
15. "Obama: Don't Jump to Conclusions," CBS News, November 6, 2009, http://www.cbsnews.com/stories/2009/11/06/national/main5551286.shtml (accessed July 29, 2010).
16. "Flight 253 Hero Recounts Thwarting Christmas Bombing Attempt," CNN.com, December 30, 2009, http://www.cnn.com/2009/US/12/30/terror.passenger.account/index.html (accessed July 29, 2010).
17. Ibid.
18. Dan Murphy, "Al Qaeda Ties of Umar Farouk Abdulmutallab: How Deep Do They Go?" *Christian Science Monitor*, December 28, 2009, http://www.csmonitor.com/World/Global-News/2009/1229/Al-Qaeda-ties-of-Umar-Farouk-Abdulmutallab-How-deep-do-they-go (accessed July 29, 2010) and http://www.cbsnews.com/stories/2010/02/04/national/main6174780.shtml (accessed July 29, 2010).
19. Armen Keteyian, "U.S. Intel Lapses Helped Abdulmutallab, CBS News.com, December 29, 2009, http://www.cbsnews.com/stories/2009/12/29/cbsnews_investigates/main6035647.shtml (accessed July 29, 2010).
20. Brian Ross and Kirit Radia, "Northwest 253: Evidence of Missed Signals Mounts," ABC News, December 29, 2009, http://abcnews.go.com/Blotter/northwest-253-obama-hits-missed-signals/story?id=9442883 (accessed July 29, 2010).
21. "Cheney Says Obama Initially Said Christmas Day Bomber Was an 'Isolated Extremist,'" February 14, 2010, http://www.politifact.com/truth-o-meter/statements/2010/feb/15/dick-cheney/cheney-says-obama-initially-said-christmas-day-bom/ (accessed July 29, 2010).
22. Benjamin F. Carlson, "Janet Napolitano: 'The System Worked.'" *Atlantic Wire*, December 27, 2009, http://www.theatlanticwire.com/features/view/feature/Janet-Napolitano-The-System-Worked-519 (accessed July 29, 2010).
23. Andrew Johnson and Emily Dugan, "Wealthy, Quiet, Unassuming: the Christmas Day Bomb Suspect," *Independent* (UK), December 27, 2009, http://www.independent.co.uk/news/

world/americas/wealthy-quiet-unassuming-the-christmas-day-bomb-suspect-1851090.html (accessed July 29, 2010).

24. Bobby Ghosh, "Domestic-terrorism Incidents Hit a Peak in 2009," *Time*, December 23, 2009, http://www.time.com/time/nation/article/0,8599,1949329,00.html (accessed July 29, 2010).

25. Ibid.

26. "Going Jihad," RAND, November 2009, http://www.rand.org/pubs/testimonies/2009/RAND_CT336.pdf (accessed July 29, 2010).

27. "Radical Islam? What's That?" May 13, 2009, http://www.powerlineblog.com/archives/2010/05/026287.php (accessed July 29, 2010).

28. "Counterterror Adviser Defends Jihad as 'Legitimate Tenet of Islam,'" Fox News, May 27, 2010, http://www.foxnews.com/politics/2010/05/27/counterterror-adviser-defends-jihad-legitimate-tenet-islam/ (accessed July 29, 2010).

29. "Remarks by Assistant to the President for Homeland Security and Counterterrorism John Brennan at CSIS," The White House, May 26, 2010, http://www.whitehouse.gov/the-press-office/remarks-assistant-president-homeland-security-and-counterterrorism-john-brennan-csi (accessed July 29, 2010).

30. Daniel Pipes, "[Al Hudaybiya and] Lessons from the Prophet Muhammad's Diplomacy," September 1999, http://www.danielpipes.org/316/al-hudaybiya-and-lessons-from-the-prophet-muhammads (accessed July 29, 2010).

31. "Introduction to the Hamas Charter," MidEastWeb.org, August 18, 1988, http://www.mideastweb.org/hamas.htm (accessed July 29, 2010).

32. Bernard Lewis, *The Crisis of Islam* (New York: Random House, 2004), 135.

Chapter 6

1. Rick Klein, "Obama's Evolving Take on Meeting with Iran," ABC News, May 20, 2008, http://abcnews.go.com/Politics/Vote2008/story?id=4896002&page=1 (accessed September 1, 2010).

2. Read more: http://www.nydailynews.com/opinions/2008/05

/21/2008-05-21_obama_needs_a_quick_refresher_course_in_.
html#ixzz0yTSJSF4I (accessed September 1, 2010).

3. SHULTZ: IF ARMS TREATY ISN'T GAINED, "SO BE IT," Herald
Wire Services, June 16, 1983.
4. Nathan Thrall and Jesse James Wilkins, "Kennedy Talked,
Krushchev Triumphed," *New York Times*, May 22, 2008, http://
www.nytimes.com/2008/05/22/opinion/22thrall.html (accessed
September 1, 2010).
5. Christopher Hitchens. *Hitch-22* (New York City: Hachette Book
Group, 2010), 266.
6. "Country Report 2010 Edition: Iran," http://www.freedomhouse
.org/template.cfm?page=22&year=2010&country=7842 (accessed
September 3, 2010).
7. See http://www.freedomhouse.org/template.cfm?page=22&year=
2010&country=7842 and http://www.freedomhouse.org/template
.cfm?page=363&year=2008&country=7413 (accessed September
3, 2010).
8. Matthias Kuntzel, "Ahmadinejad's Demons," *New Republic*,
April 24, 2006, http://www.matthiaskuentzel.de/contents/
ahmadinejads-demons (accessed September 3, 2010).
9. Chris Kraul and Sebastian Rotella, "Fears of a Hezbollah Presence
in Venezuela," *Los Angeles Times*, April 27, 2008, http://articles
.latimes.com/2008/aug/27/world/fg-venezterror27 (accessed
September 3, 2010).
10. James Glanz, "U.S. Presents Evidence of Iranian Weapons in
Iraq," *New York Times*, February 11, 2007, http://www.nytimes
.com/2007/02/11/world/middleeast/11cnd-weapons.html
(accessed September 3, 2010).
11. George Jahn, "UN Nuke Agency Worried Iran May Be Working
on Arms," ABC News, February18, 2010. http://abcnews.go.com/
International/wireStory?id=9875227 (accessed September 3, 2010).
12. James Phillips, "Iran's Nuclear Program: What Is Known and
Unknown," The Heritage Foundation, March 26, 2010, http://
www.heritage.org/research/reports/2010/03/iran-s-nuclear-
program-what-is-known-and-unknown#_ftn4 (accessed
September 3, 2010).

13. Ibid.
14. Mark Mazzetti and David E. Sanger. "U.S. Persuades Israel That Iran's Nuclear Threat Is Not Imminent," *New York Times*, August 18, 2010, http://www.nytimes.com/2010/08/20/world/middleeast/20policy.html (accessed September 3, 2010).
15. Ibid.
16. "Prepared Testimony of Dr. Michael A. Ledeen to the Senate Homeland Security and Governmental Affairs Subcommittee on Federal Financial Management, Government Information, and International Security," http://hsgac.senate.gov/public/index.cfm?FuseAction=Files.View&FileStore_id=f45b50d3-c125-45bf-9201-6b18349fc3bf- (accessed September 3, 2010).
17. Mark Silva, "Obama's Persian New Year Note to Iran," March 20, 2009, http://www.swamppolitics.com/news/politics/blog/2009/03/obamas_persian_new_year_note_t.html (accessed September 3, 2010).
18. Ibid.
19. Ibid.
20. "The View from the Gulag," *Weekly Standard*, June 11, 2004, http://www.weeklystandard.com/Content/Public/Articles/000/000/004/224ncdel.asp (accessed September 3, 2010).
21. Elie Wiesel, *Evil and Exile* (Notre Dame: University of Notre Dame Press, 1990), 130.
22. Roger Cohen, "The Making of an Iran Policy," *New York Times*, August 2, 2009, http://www.nytimes.com/2009/08/02/magazine/02Iran-t.html?_r=1&pagewanted=print (accessed September 3, 2010).
23. David Blair, "Iran Election: Barack Obama Refuses to 'Meddle' over Protests," *Telegraph* (UK), June 17, 2009, http://www.telegraph.co.uk/news/worldnews/middleeast/iran/5556155/Iran-election-Barack-Obama-refuses-to-meddle-over-protests.html (accessed September 3, 2010).
24. "Obama Condemns 'Unjust' Violence," BBC News, June 23, 2009, http://news.bbc.co.uk/2/hi/8115232.stm (accessed September 3, 2010).
25. Seth Leibsohn, "The U.S. Doesn't Want to Be Seen as Meddling,"

National Review, June 16, 2009, http://www.nationalreview.com/corner/183399/u-s-doesnt-want-be-seen-meddling/seth-leibsohn (accessed September 3, 2010).

26. Mark Landler, "A New Iran Overture, with Hot Dogs," *New York Times*, June 2, 2009, http://www.nytimes.com/2009/06/02/world/02diplo.html (accessed September 3, 2010).

27. "Iran Announces Plans for New Nuclear Sites," CBS News, http://www.cbsnews.com/stories/2010/08/16/world/main6777465.shtml (accessed November 19, 2010).

28. "Iran Unveils 'Ambassador of Death' Bomber," MSNBC.com, August 23, 2010, http://www.msnbc.msn.com/id/38804551/ns/world_news-mideastn_africa/ (accessed August 24, 2010).

29. Norman Podhoretz, "The Case for Bombing Iran," *Commentary Magazine*, June 2007, http://www.commentarymagazine.com/viewarticle.cfm/the-case-for-bombing-iran-10882 (accessed September 3, 2010).

Chapter 7

1. "Growing Number of Americans Say Obama Is a Muslim," Pew Research Center Publications, August 19, 2010, http://pewresearch.org/pubs/1701/poll-obama-muslim-christian-church-out-of-politics-political-leaders-religious (accessed August 29, 2010).

2. "Obama Egypt Speech: VIDEO, Full Text," *Huffington Post*, June 4, 2009, http://www.huffingtonpost.com/2009/06/04/obama-egypt-speech-video_n_211216.html (accessed August 29, 2010).

3. Jake Tapper and Sunlen Miller, "The Emergence of President Obama's Muslim Roots," ABC News, June 2, 2009, http://blogs.abcnews.com/politicalpunch/2009/06/abc-news-jake-tapper-and-sunlen-miller-report-the-other-day-we-heard-a-comment-from-a-white-house-aide-that-neverwould-have.html (accessed August 29, 2010).

4. Sam Stein, "Obama 'Bow' to Saudis: CNN Reporter Asks White House to Clarify," *Huffington Post*, April 9, 2009, http://www.huffingtonpost.com/2009/04/09/obama-bow-to-saudis-cnn-r_n_185281.html (accessed August 29, 2010).

5. Reuel Marc Gerecht, "Islam: Unmentionable in D.C.," *New Republic*, July 14, 2010, http://www.tnr.com/blog/foreign-policy/76249/islam-unmentionable-in-dc (accessed August 29, 2010).

6. Ibid.

7. "To Bigotry No Sanction, to Persecution No Assistance," Jewish Virtual Library, http://www.jewishvirtuallibrary.org/jsource/US-Israel/bigotry.html (accessed August 29, 2010).

8. Ibid. Verse: Micah 4:4.

9. "Atlas Exclusive! Ground Zero Mosque Imam Feisal's Extremism Exposed . . ." August 23, 2010, http://atlasshrugs2000.typepad .com/atlas_shrugs/2010/08/explosive-in-faisals-own-words.html (accessed August 29, 2010).

10. "Reactions to Sheikh Al-Qaradhawi's Fatwa Calling for the Abduction and Killing of American Civilians in Iraq," Memri, October 6, 2004, http://www.memri.org/report/en/0/0/0/0/0/0/1231.htm (accessed August 29, 2010).

11. See for example, http://www.npr.org/templates/story/story .php?storyId=124494788 (accessed August 29, 2010).

12. Matthew 7:1; John 8:7; Romans 2:1; Matthew 5:39; Matthew 5:5 (KJV).

13. Raymond Ibrahim, "Are Judaism and Christianity as Violent as Islam?" Middle East Forum, Summer 2009, http://www.meforum .org/2159/are-judaism-and-christianity-as-violent-as-islam (accessed September 1, 2010).

14. David Gelernter, *Judaism: A Way of Being* (New Haven: Yale University Press, 2009), 205.

15. Melanie Phillips, *The World Turned Upside Down* (New York City: Encounter Books, 2010), 162.

16. Micah 4:5 (NIV).

17. Koran 9.29.

18. *The Book of Faith (Kitab Al-Iman)*, Center for Muslim-Jewish Engagement, http://www.usc.edu/schools/college/crcc/engagement/resources/texts/muslim/hadith/muslim/001.smt .html (accessed August 29, 2010); Sahih Muslim, Book 001, Number 0030.

19. Rabbi Louis Jacobs, "The Death Penalty in Jewish Tradition," http://www.myjewishlearning.com/life/Life_Events/Death_and_Mourning/About_Death_and_Mourning/Death_Penalty.shtml (accessed August 29, 2010).
20. Zeff Rabbi Leff, *Shemoneh Esrei* (Southfield, MO: Targum Press, 2008), 245.
21. Barbara Bradley Hagerty, "Is the Bible More Violent Than the Quran?" NPR, March 18, 2010, http://www.npr.org/templates/story/story.php?storyId=124494788 (accessed August 29, 2010).
22. Ibid.
23. 1 Chronicles 22:8.
24. Quoted in: William J. Bennett, *Why We Fight* (Washington, DC: Regnery Publishing, 2003), 90.
25. Bernard Lewis, *The Crisis of Islam* (New York: Random House), 137.
26. David Bukay, "The Religions Foundations of Suicide Bombings," Middle East Forum, Fall 2006, http://www.meforum.org/1003/the-religious-foundations-of-suicide-bombings#_ftnref23 (accessed August 29, 2010).
27. Judea Pearl, "Undercurrents Below the Ground Zero Mosque," *Jerusalem Post*, August 28, 2010, http://www.jpost.com/Opinion/Op-EdContributors/Article.aspx?id=186290 (accessed September 1, 2010).
28. M. Zuhdi Jasser, "AIFD Brief: MPAC/ISNA Counterterrorism Video Deceptive," AIDF, August 27, 2010, http://www.aifdemocracy.org/news.php?id=6111 (accessed September 1, 2010).
29. Imam Zaid Shakir, "Responding to the Fort Hood Tragedy," November 13, 2009, http://seekersguidance.org/blog/2009/11/responding-to-the-fort-hood-tragedy-imam-zaid-shakir/ (accessed September 1, 2010).
30. Laurie Goodstein, "U.S. Muslim Clerics Seek a Modern Middle Ground," *New York Times*, June 18, 2006, http://www.nytimes.com/2006/06/18/us/18imams.html?_r=1&pagewanted=4 (accessed September 1, 2010).
31. Tara Bahrampour, "U.S. Muslim Leaders Make Push to Unify Their Communities," *Washington Post*, August 31, 2010, http://www.washingtonpost.com/wp-dyn/content/article/2010/08/30/

AR2010083005326_pf.html (accessed September 1, 2010).

32. "Salam al-Marayati," IPT, http://www.investigativeproject.org/ profile/114#_ftnref8 (accessed September 1, 2010).

33. Joseph Picard, "Islamic Group Issues PSAs to Combat Bigotry," *International Business Times*, August 31, 2010, http://www.ibtimes .com/articles/47919/20100831/mosque-islam.htm (accessed September 1, 2010).

34. "Nihad Awad," IPT, http://www.investigativeproject.org/ profile/113 (accessed September 1, 2010).

35. Reuel Marc Gerecht, "What Is Moderate Islam?" *New Republic*, August 11, 2010, http://www.tnr.com/blog/foreign-policy/76929/ what-moderate-islam (accessed September 3, 2010).

36. Joshua Gilder, "Why Islamic Moderates Are So Scarce," *National Review*, September 2, 2010, http://www.nationalreview.com/ articles/print/245415 (accessed September 5, 2010).

37. Jon Meacham, "Let Reformation Begin at Ground Zero," *Newsweek*, August 28, 2010, http://www-prod-1948660122.us-east-1.elb .amazonaws.com/2010/08/28/meacham-let-reformation-begin-at-ground-zero.html# (accessed October 31, 2010).

38. Bret Stephens, "Our 'Moderate Muslim' Problem," *Wall Street Journal*, August 17, 2010, http://online.wsj.com/article/SB1000142 4052748704868604575433214247852860.html?mod=googlenews_ wsj (accessed September 1, 2010).

39. Gerecht, "What Is Moderate Islam?"

Chapter 8

1. Tony Blair, *A Journey: My Political Life* (New York City: Knopf, 2010), 348.

2. Ibid.

3. "UCSD Muslim Student Association Member Admits She Wants Another Holocaust," May 11, 2010, http://joshuapundit.blogspot .com/2010/05/ucsd-muslim-student-association-member.html (accessed September 1, 2010).

4. Andrew C. McCarthy, "The Tolerant Pose," *National Review*, August 17, 2010, http://www.nationalreview.com/ articles/243899/tolerant-pose-andrew-c-mccarthy (accessed September 1, 2010).

5. Ibid.
6. "Legislative Fact Sheet: U.S.-Muslim World Relations," CAIR, October 8, 2001, http://www.cair.com/GovernmentRelations/ IssuesandLegislation/USMuslimWorldRelations.aspx (accessed September 5, 2010).
7. "The Council on American-Islamic Relations (CAIR): CAIR Exposed," IPT, http://www.investigativeproject.org/documents/ misc/122.pdf (accessed September 1, 2010).
8. "Open Minds: Lessons from Arabia's Past," *Sunday Times* (UK), December 21, 2008, http://www.timesonline.co.uk/tol/news/ world/middle_east/article5358194.ece (accessed September 1, 2010).
9. "Rima Khalaf Drops a Bomb," Worldpress.org, July 4, 2002, http://www.worldpress.org/mideast/663.cfm (accessed October 4, 2010).
10. Glenn Frankel, "Religious Moderates Meet with Blair to Address Attacks," *Washington Post*, June 20, 2005, A4.
11. Tony Blair, "Tony Blair Takes on the World," *Wall Street Journal*, September 4, 2010, http://online.wsj.com/article/ SB10001424052748704206804575467673238817104. html?KEYWORDS=%22tony+blair%22 (accessed September 4, 2010).
12. Michale B. Mukasey, "America's most wanted," *Wall Street Journal*, January 22, 2011, http://online.wsj.com/article/SB10001424052 7487035834045760799304943323352.html?mod=WSJ_newsreel_ opinion (accessed January 25, 2011).
13. Tawfik Hamid, "Islam Needs to Prove It's a Religion of Peace," *Wall Street Journal*, March 9, 2009, http://online.wsj.com/article/ NA_WSJ_PUB:SB123654552575064501.html (accessed September 3, 2010).
14. Nina Shea and Bonnie Alldredge, "Saudi Textbooks: Still Teaching Hatred," *National Review*, June 29, 2010, http://www. nationalreview.com/articles/print/243357 (accessed September 3, 2010).
15. Nina Shea, "Ground Zero Mosque: Who's in Charge?" *National Review*, August 9, 2010, http://www.nationalreview.com/articles/ print/243639 (accessed September 3, 2010).

16. Angelo M. Codevilla, "Why We Don't Win," The Claremont Institute, May 10, 2010, http://www.claremont.org/publications/crb/id.1678/article_detail.asp (accessed September 3, 2010).

Epilogue

1. Mark Steyn, "A Victory for Multiculti over Common Sense," *Telegraph* (UK), July 19, 2005, http://www.telegraph.co.uk/comment/personal-view/3618488/A-victory-for-multiculti-over-common-sense.html (accessed September 1, 2010).

2. David S. Broder, "Harry Potter and Our Forgotten History," *Washington Post*, July 28, 2005, http://www.washingtonpost.com/wp-dyn/content/article/2005/07/28/AR2005072800213.html (accessed September 1, 2010).

3. William Damon, "Teaching Students to Count Their Blessings," http://www.edexcellence.net/detail/news.cfm?news_id=65&pubsubid=724#724 (accessed September 5, 2010).

4. C. S. Lewis, *The Abolition of Man* (New York: Macmillan, 1965), 35.

5. Ibid (emphasis added).

6. "Lyceum Address," http://showcase.netins.net/web/creative/lincoln/speeches/lyceum.htm (accessed October 4, 2010).

INDEX

A

Abbas, Abu, 37
Abdulmutallab, Umar Farouk, 75, 77
absolutism, moral vs. immoral, 146
academic community, support for
    Ramadan, 40
Achille Lauro, hijacking of, 37
ACLU, 40
Afghanistan
    Bush credit for war in, 30
    public support for U.S. military
        in, 3–4
    U.S. efforts in, 132
    U.S. support for mujahedeen, 25
Ahmadinejad, Mahmoud, xiii, 89
    announcement of election, 97
    arming for war and destruction,
        100
Ahmed, Farooque, xi–xii
Akiba, Rabbi, 114
Alexander, Lamar, 144
Amanpour, Christiane, xii
American Academy of Religion, 40
American Association of University
    Professors, 40
American goodwill, 29
American history, need to teach, 144
American hostages in Iran, 88
American identity, need for, 142
American Islamic Forum for
    Democracy, 118
American left, and Bush description
    of enemy, 31

American Muslims, mainstream
    leadership groups, 122–125
Americans for Victory Over
    Terrorism, 3, 4
anger, 136
Anti-Defamation League, 50–51
antiwar contingent, 66
"anxious propitiation," 22
appeasement, 22, 77, 78, 100, 104
Arafat, Yasser, 24, 77, 82
Armitage, Richard, 44
Ash'arites, 124
assembly, freedom of, 89
al-Awlaki, Anwar, 8–9, 76, 77
Azariah, Eliezer ben, 114
Al-Azhar University, 71

B

al-Banna, Hasan, 41
Barone, Michael, on Hard and Soft
    America, 11
Basiji movement, 90
Bawer, Bruce, 43*n*
Beirut, 22
    bombings, 44
Berlin Wall, 87
Berman, Paul, 38, 39, 40, 42
Bible
    Micah, 107–108, 113
    Old Testament, 112, 115
    violence in, 111, 112
bin Laden, Osama, 7, 40, 77, 81–82,
    132

Index

declaration of war against U.S., 22
  lesson learned, 25
Blair, Tony, 129–130, 137, 138–139
blame, 138
"blame America first" attitude, 67
Blitzer, Wolf, 59
bombings
  Beirut, 44
  Kuwait American embassy, 24
  moderate Islam denunciation,
    119
  suicide, by Hezbollah, 44
  Times Square attempt, 78
  World Trade Center in 1993, 25n
bowing to foreign leader, 105n
Bradley, Ed, 49
Bremer, Jerry, 3
Brennan, John, 103
  comments on jihad, 81
Brezhnev, Leonid, 34
Burlingame, Debra, 135–136
Bush, George W., 106
  address at mosque, 30
  credit for wars in Afghanistan and
    Iraq, 30
  rhetoric of, 60
  second inaugural address, 59
  speech to Congress joint session,
    26–27
Bush administration, 57
  examples of confusion in, 31

C
Casey, George, 5, 10–11
change, source for, 47
chemical weapons, Hussein's use, 35
Chertoff, Michael, 73
children
  education on Western ethics, 144
  treatment by Iran, 90
China, Nixon and, 87
Choudary, Anjem, on being Muslim,
  xiii

Christianity, 125–126
  and violence, 111–116
Church of Latter Day Saints, 126
Churchill, Winston, 26, 137
clarity, 138–142
classified national security wartime
  intelligence, disclosure of, 38
clear thought and language,
  problems of, 57–58
Clinton, Bill, 24, 63
Clinton, Hillary, 43, 99–100n
closed societies, 134
CNN, firing of Nasr, 43
Codevilla, Angelo, 141
Commonwealth Club (San
  Francisco), Gore speech at, 33–34
conspiracy theories, 134
"Cordoba Initiative," 48
corrupted language, 61
costs of war, appreciation for, 65
Council on American Islamic
  Relations, 31, 123, 133–134
crisis of will, 15–18
Crose, Bradley, 65
crusade, Bush use of term, 31
Cuba, Obama willingness to meet
  with leaders, 86
Cuban Missile Crisis, 87
cultural health, indicators, 19–20
culture of grievance, ending,
  135–138
Cuomo, Mario, xiiin

D
Damon, William, 145
Dauber, Cori, 65
David (Old Testament king), 115
daydreams, danger of, 77–81
death penalty, 114
defense of the West and America,
  143–144
Democrats, 62–63
diversity, 10, 54, 144

Index

domestic terrorism, factors
motivating, 14

E

education, diversity in, 10
Egypt, Obama travel to, 71
Emerson, Ralph Waldo, 61
Emerson, Steve, 30, 40, 48n
emotional empathy, from leaders, 136
empathy, absence of, 21
empathy inflation, 136–137
enemy, 61, 66–67, 132, 148
  Bush description of, 30–31
  description, 139–140
  identifying, 117
  need to confront, 141
evil, visibility of, 20
extremism, 60–61

F

Fadlallah, Sayyed Mohammed
  Hussein, 43, 44
  statement about women, 45
Fakih, Rima, 29, 54
Fatah, Tarek, 53
Feaver, Peter, 65
Foner, Eric, 20n
Fort Hood shooting
  analysis of cause, 16–17
  Pentagon investigation, 12–15
  Shakir statement after, 120–121
  Soldier Readiness Center, 1
Foundation for the Defense of
  Democracies, 106
Foxman, Abraham, 50–51
Freedom House, 30, 89
freedom, need for education about,
  145
freedom of assembly, 89
Friedman, Thomas, 45–46, 47
fundamentalism, 141, 146
Fundamentalist Mormon Church,
  126

G

Gelernter, David, 111, 112
generosity, 29
Gerecht, Reuel Marc, 106, 123
Germany, U.S. war against, 34n
Gilder, Joshua, 124
Global War on Terror (GWOT), 74
"golden age of Islam," 124
"good Muslim," 126–127
Gorbachev, Mikhail, 87
Gore, Al, 33–34, 38
Gregory, David, 10
grievances of radical Islam, 143
Gromyko, Andrei, xiiin
ground zero mosque, 48–55, 109
  Muslim opponents to, 53
  Obama on, 51–52
  potential impact, 133
Guantanamo detainees, trial, xiv

H

Hadith, 114
Hamas, 41, 134
  charter, 82
  Hussein support of, 37
  Iran financial support for, 90
  Rauf and, 49–50
Hamid, Tawfik, 140
Hasan, Nidal, 1, 5–8, 74n, 77
  opposition to war on terror in
    Afghanistan and Iraq, 5–6
  Peters on, 15
  PowerPoint presentation by, 6–7
  public nature of activities and
    statements, 10
  response to, 121
  suicide pact, 7–9
hate crimes, statistics, 29
Havel, Vaclav, 98
heresy, 114n
hesitation, rhetoric of, 71
Hezbollah, 24
  and American casualties, 44

Iran financial support for, 90
Hinderaker, John, 39
Hitchens, Christopher, 38, 88
on Hussein, 36–37
Holder, Eric, congressional
testimony, 78–80
Homeland Security, secretary of, 73
honesty, in problem recognition,
17
hope, United States and, 98
Horowitz, David, 131
Hughes, Karen, 58
human rights violations, in Iraq,
35
Hussein, Saddam, 26n, 35, 62, 63
barbarism of, 36
Iraq without, 135
and terrorism, 64
al-Husseini, Haj Amin, 41

I
Ibrahim, Raymond, 112
inaction, 22–26
intellectual class, 21–22
International Atomic Energy Agency,
91
Iran
as potential nuclear power, 83
presidential election in 2009,
97–99
restrictions and abuses, 89
rise and rule of mullahs, 88–90
U.S. intelligence in, 99
uranium enrichment program,
91, 100
Iranian people
help sought by, 93
Obama's message to, 94–95
Iraq, 72
Bush credit for war in, 30
human rights violations in, 35
U.S. efforts in, 132
war protesters, 38

weapons of mass destruction, 35
without Hussein, 135
Islam
ambivalence, 118–122
golden age, 124
Hasan's allegiance to, 6
moderate, 110, 123, 131, 137
need for reform, 129, 139
Orthodox, 54
radical, 103, 126, 137, 143
as "religion of peace," 27–28, 103,
106–107, 118–119
response to threat, 136
spectrum, 130
*Islam, the West and the Challenges of
Modernity* (Ramadan), 39
Islamic Center of Washington,
statement about, 27–28
Islamic community center in NY, 48
Islamic Forum for Democracy, 71
Islamic Jihad
Hussein support of, 37
Iran financial support for, 90
Islamic violence, 116–118
Islamists, describing enemy as, 82
Israel, 72, 113, 123, 132–133

J
Jackson, Robert, 9
Jacoby, Jeff, 24
Jasser, Zuhdi, 54n, 71, 118–119, 129
Jenkins, Phillip, 115
Jesus Christ, 111
Jewish morality, 112
Jewish scriptures, violence in, 113
jihad, 81–82, 106, 117
jihadist Web sites, 8
John Paul II (pope), 52
Johnson, Scott, 39
journalist community
disclosure of classified national
security wartime intelligence, 38
reaction to Nasr firing, 45

Judaism
cities of refuge, 114
and converts, 113
Orthodox, 126
and violence, 111–116
just war, 112

K
Kean, Tom, xiii*n*
Kennedy, Brian, 100
Kennedy, John F., 98
Kennedy-Khrushchev summit
(1961), 87
Kerry, John, 60
Khan, A.Q., 91
Khomeini, Ayatollah, 88
Khrushchev, Nikita, 87
King, Martin Luther Jr., 125–126
"Letter from Birmingham Jail,"
60–61
Kinsley, Michael, 50, 51
Koran
vs. Bible, violence, 111
commands to jihad and physical
violence, 117
Hasan quote from, 6–7
on non-believers, 113–114
violence in, 115
Krauthammer, Charles, 3
Kuwait, 26*n*
American embassy bombing, 24

L
language
corrupted, 61
lack of moral vocabulary of war,
64–68
leaders, emotional empathy from, 136
leadership, lack of, 61–64
Lebanon, U.S. pullout, 23–24
Ledeen, Michael, 90, 93–94, 99, 100
Lewis, Bernard, 22, 25, 82, 117, 141
Lewis, C.S., 146

Screwtape Letters, 122
Lichenstein, Charles, xiii*n*
Lincoln, Abraham, 18, 105*n*, 137
Lyceum speech, 147–148
listening, 58
London, terrorist attacks, 137

M
man-caused disasters, 73
Manji, Irshad, 125
Al-Marayati, Salam, 122–123
Marine barracks bombing (1983), 23
Martin, Roland, 50, 51
McCarthy, Andrew, 39, 63, 131
McCullough, David, 144
Meacham, Jon, and reform, 125
Meet the Press, 10
Meyers, Richard, 59–60
Micah, 107–108, 113
Middle East, state-controlled media,
134
Miller, John, 23
minesweepers, children as, 90
Mirengoff, Paul, 39
Miss USA, 29
moderate Islam, 110
in America, 131
American leaders, 137
differences in different countries,
123
Mohammed, Khalid Sheikh, 61–62
Moore, Michael, 39
moral absolutism, vs. immoral, 146
moral clarity, 136
mosques
at ground zero, 48–55, 109, 133
sources of funding, 48*n*
in U.S., 52–53
mourning death of leaders, 47–48
Mubarak, Hosni, 71
Mughniyeh, Imad, 44
mujahedeen in Afghanistan, U.S.
support for, 25

multicultural sophistication, nonjudgmental views, 46
Muslim American Public Affairs Council, 122–123
Muslim Brotherhood, 41
Muslim Canadian Congress, 53
Muslim Public Affairs Council, video on issue of violent extremism, 120
Muslims
  Bush on respect for faith of, 27
  Choudary on characteristics of, xiii
  duty of nonviolent, 82
  fear of, xii
  fundamentalism, 23
  reformist, 131
Muslims in America
  civil liberties of, 9
  conditions after 9/11, 28–30
  mainstream leadership groups, 122–125
  moderate, 131
  rights, 133
al-Mutawakkil, Caliph Ja'afar, 124

N
Napolitano, Janet, 76
  testimony before Congress, 73
Nasr, Octavia, 43, 47
Nasrallah, Sheikh Hassan, 44
National Assessment of Educational Progress, 144
national identity, 144
neutrality, in Iran elections, 98
neutron initiator, Iran testing of, 91
New Republic, 106
New York Times, 6, 39, 45, 52, 59, 60, 71, 92, 97, 99
Nidal, Abu, 37
Nitze, Paul, 87
Nixon, Richard, 87
non-Muslims, right to call for defense of West and America, 129

nonviolent Muslims, duty of, 82
Nordlinger Jay, 100
Northwest Flight 253, attempted bombing, 75
Notre Dame, professorship offer to Ramadan, 39

O
Obama, Barack, xi, 38
  address on war on Islamic terror, 70
  after Iran election, 97–98
  on evil, 66–67
  on ground zero mosque, 51–52
  on his knowledge of Islam, 104–105
  inaugural address, 69–70
  and Iran, 86–88
  on Islam as religion of peace, 103
  message to Iranian people, 94–95
  statement after 9/11, 21, 67
  statement after attempted plane bombing, 76
  statement after Fort Hood shooting, 75
  trip to Middle East, 71–72
Obama administration, xiv, 57, 67
  on Iran nuclear development, 92
  position on Afghanistan, 4
Office of Management and Budget, e-mail memo, 74
Old Testament, 115
  violence in, 112
Orszag, Peter, 75
Orthodox Islam, 54
Orthodox Judaism, 126
Overseas Contingency Operation, 74

P
pacification, 77
pacifism, Koran and, 115
Palestine Liberation Organization (PLO), 24

Index

"Park51," 48
peace
  Islam as religion of, 27–28, 103,
    106–107, 118–119
  path to, 125–127
Pearl, Daniel, 119
Pearl, Judea, 119–120
Pearl Harbor, 2
Pelosi, Nancy, 38
PEN, 40
Pentagon. *See* U.S. Department of
  Defense
Peters, Ralph, 12–13, 15
Petraeus, David, xi
Pew Research Center, 104
Phares, Walid, 3
Phillips, James, 91
Phillips, Melanie, 113
Pipes, Daniel, 40*n*
pluralism, 125
Podhoretz, Norman, 23
political Judaism, 113
political leadership, and crisis of
  will, 17
political left, opposition to military
  action, 35
political religion, 137, 146–149
politics, 65
Pollack, Kenneth, 36
polygamy, 125, 126
Ponnuru, Ramesh, 62
power, Obama on, 69
preemptive, 34
Press Club, 59–60
propaganda, 134
*Protecting the Force: Lessons from Fort
  Hood*, 12–15
protests, against Iraq war, 38
Protocols of the Elders of Zion, 30
public diplomacy, undersecretary
  of state for, Senate confirmation
  hearings, 57–58
public opinion after 9/11, 3

public support
  for military operations, 65
  for U.S. military in Afghanistan,
    3–4

Q
al-Qaeda, 24
  responsibility for 9/11, xiii
al-Qaeda in Iraq, 37
al-Qaeda in Mesopotamia, 37
Qaradawi, Sheikh Yusuf, 41
al-Qaradawi, Yusuf, 110
Quran. *See* Koran
Qutb, Sayyid, 41

R
radical Islam, 103, 126, 137
  grievances of, 143
Ramadan, Tariq, 39
  view of women, 42
RAND Corporation, 78
Rauf, Imam Feisal Abdul, 48,
  109–110
  defenses of, 51
Raza, Raheel, 53
Reagan, Ronald, 70, 86–87
  on Soviet Union as evil empire, 31,
    95–96
  stand against Soviet Union, 23
reformed Islam, need for, 129
reformist Muslims, 131
religion, 147
  respectful treatment as American
    goal, 107
resolve
  after 9/11, 19
  weakening of, 21
respect for Muslim faith, Bush on, 27
rhetoric, 18
  in democracy, 65–66
  of hesitation and self-doubt, 71
  of tolerance, 28
Ridge, Tom, 73

Rieff, Philip, 136
"Rightwing Extremism: Current
    Economic and Political
    Climate Fueling Resurgence in
    Radicalization and Recruitment,
    73–74
Roosevelt, Franklin, 2, 31, 137
root causes, debate of, 136
Rove, Karl, 62
    apology, 63
Rubin, Michael, 100

S
Said, Edward, 20*n*
Salon.com, 39
Samore, Gary, 92
Sarkozy, Nicolas, 42
Saudi Arabia
    king, and Obama, 105
    Muslims in, 123
    Obama travel to, 71
Schuringa, Jasper, 75
Screwtape Letters (Lewis), 122
self-condemnation, beginnings of, 33
self-defense, abnegating
    responsibilities of, 15
self-doubt
    about America, 4
    rhetoric of, 71
"self-radicalization," 14
Senate Select Committee on
    Intelligence, 2004 report on
    Hussein, 64
September 11 attacks
    interviews with al-Awlaki after, 8
    Islam and, 116
    Obama statement after, 67
    public opinion after, 3
    resolve following, 19
    response to, 21
    U.S. response, 2–3
Serbia, 34*n*
Shah of Iran, 88

Shahzad, Faisal, xii, 78
Shakir, Imam Zaid, 120
Sharansky, Natan, 96
Sharia (Islamic law), 89, 125
Sheehan, Cindy, 39
Shulchan Aruch, 113, 114
Shultz, George, 24, 87
60 Minutes, 48*n*
Smith, Lamar, 78–80
SOA (Soldier of Allah), 8
social studies, vs. history teaching,
    144–145
Soldier of Allah (SOA), 8
Solomon (Old Testament king), 115
Somalia, 22–23
Sontag, Susan, 20*n*
Soviet Union
    as evil empire, 95–96
    policies of aggression in
        Afghanistan, 34
    U.S. response to, 93
speech, restrictions in Iran, 89
Der Spiegel, 73
Srebrenica, 54
Stephens, Bret, 100
Stethem, Robert, 44
Steyn, Mark, 74*n*, 144
stoning women, Ramadan on, 42
suicide bombings, by Hezbollah, 44
surrender, 3–5
sympathizers, 130

T
Taheri, Amir, 116
Talmud, 113, 114
taqiyya, art of, 40
Tarfon, Rabbi, 114
terminology, 74, 77–78
terror front, news from, xi, xiv
terrorism
    causes and justification, 138
    domestic, factors motivating, 14
    justification, 49

term use by administration
officials, 73
terrorist attacks
reasons for attempts, 79–80
worldwide in 2009, 78n
terrorists
legal community defense of rights,
38
need for isolating, 141
Time, 39, 53
Times Square, bomb in, 78
To Be a European Muslim (Ramadan),
39
tolerance, 54, 133
rhetoric of, 28
Touro Synagogue, Washington letter
to, 107
Transportation Safety
Administration, "no-fly" list, 76
Tsongas, Paul, 87
Turkey, Obama travel to, 71
tyrants, attack plans, 132

U
United Nations, 105
Ahmadinejad address to, xiii
United States
professors' persuasion of students,
43n
Rauf view as accessory to crime,
49
show of force in Kuwait, 26n
U.S. Department of Defense
"Follow-on Review" with "Final
Recommendations" on Fort
Hood, 15–16
investigation of Fort Hood
massacre, 12–15
U.S. government, bin Laden on
evidence of decline, 23
U.S. military, 11
actions on behalf of Muslims,
58–59

interest in joining after 9/11,
19
public support, 65

V
Venezuela
Hezbollah in, 90
Obama willingness to meet with
leaders, 86
Vietnam, body bag syndrome, 65
violence
Christian and Jewish, 111–116
Islamic, 116–118
in Koran, 117
perspectives on reasons for, 13
violent extremism, 60
vision, of nation, 62

W
Waite, Terry, 44
war, lack of moral vocabulary of,
64–68
war on Islamic terror, Obama
address on, 70
war on terrorism, 59–60
war weariness, 61
Warren, Rick, 66
Washington, George, 107, 141
Washington Post, 6, 50, 74, 137
weapons of mass destruction, Bush
administration and, 63
Weinberger, Caspar, 23
Western culture, 136
Wiesel, Elie, 96
Williams, Juan, xii
Wilson, Joe, 39
women
Fadlallah statement about, 45
Ramadan's view of, 42
Woolsey, James, 3
workforce, diversity in, 10
World Trade Center
bombing in 1993, 25n

mosque planned near, 48–55, 109, 133

World War II, 34n, 70

Wright, Jeremiah, 20–21n

Wright, Lawrence, 140

Z

al-Zarqawi, Abu, 37

al-Zawahiri, Ayman, 37, 46, 77